MW00344865

CONTENTS

CONTENTS

ACKNOWLEDGEMENTS

Our Well Crafted NC project (WellCraftedNC.com), which is focused on documenting and preserving the history of beer and brewing in North Carolina, forms the foundation for much of what you will find in this book. The seed for Well Crafted NC goes back to September 2016, when Mark Gibb, owner of Gibb's Hundred Brewing Company in downtown Greensboro, allowed us to use his taproom for an event we called "Hop into History." Hop into History was a monthly series in which we would bring archives and local history to brewery patrons through pop-up exhibits. At these Hop into History events, we met many people who worked in or had some connection to the brewing industry in the Triad region. Those people introduced us to other people, and soon our Well Crafted NC project was off to a solid start.

We are grateful to all the people in the North Carolina beer and brewing industry who sat down for oral history interviews with us, donated materials to help us preserve and share the history of the craft brewing industry today, provided us with space in their taproom for exhibits and displays and supported our work in so many other ways. Cheers go out to Jasmine Bamlet, Stuart Barnhart, Jamie Bartholomaus, Karmen Bulmer, Mark Gibb, Steve Kim, Joel McClosky, Erik Lars Myers, Anita Riley and all the members of the Triad Brewers Alliance.

All three of us work in the University Libraries at UNC Greensboro, and we have been lucky to have strong support from the University in doing this work. Thanks to Alyssa Bedrosian, Eden Bloss, Tim Bucknall, Erick

ACKNOWLEDGEMENTS

Byrd, Kathy Crowe, Emily Janke, Lori Kniffin and Terri Shelton for their support as we created and continue to expand Well Crafted NC. Financial support from the UNC Greensboro University Libraries Innovation and Enrichment Fund was vital to the start of this project. Additional support from a UNCG Faculty First Grant and a P2: Pathways and Partnerships Grant has helped us grow.

We would also like to thank all the local library, archives and museum professionals who have supported our work in various ways—by providing historical materials to aid our research, by allowing us to use photographs from their collections and by working with us on events that spotlight local beer and brewing history. Special thanks to Tiah Edmunson-Morton of Oregon State University's Oregon Hops and Brewing Archives for inspiration, support and taking the time during a pandemic to scan lots of beer magazine articles from the 1980s and 1990s.

Finally, thanks to our friends and families who provide us with support in so many ways. From Richard: Thanks to Anita and Justin for their patience with my pushing North Carolina craft beer at them, and to Franny and Daisy Mae for being the best pub doggos ever. They are missed. From David: Thanks to Mom and Dad (I miss you), to Jeff for all the beer, to Duncan for getting me home alive afterward and to Sarah, Carroll, Jennifer and the late Dan C. just for being here. From Erin: Thanks to my parents, Percy and Debbie, along with Denise, Greg, Peyton, Violet, Megan, Will and Delaney. And to Jasper for being the best corgi boy.

INTRODUCTION

The Piedmont Triad region may not be the first place that comes to mind when you think "North Carolina beer," but it was home to one of the state's earliest brewery operations, to the state's largest brewery operations and to some of the state's earliest craft brewpubs. In 2019, three of the top five highest-producing craft breweries in North Carolina were anchored in the Triad. Craft breweries have filled abandoned textile mills and tobacco warehouses across the region, providing economic growth and sparking redevelopment of Main Streets and other neighborhoods and business districts.

According to the Brewers Association, the nation's largest trade organization for the craft beer industry, North Carolina craft beer and brewing had a $2.8 million economic impact in 2019. The number of breweries in the state skyrocketed in the 2010s, and in 2019, North Carolina ranked eighth in the country for number of craft breweries with 333.[1] In many towns across the state, craft breweries have moved into former industrial sites or onto declining Main Streets, helping bring locally driven revitalization to areas needing an economic boost. It is difficult to deny the industry's expanding value to local communities and to the state.

The growing importance of craft breweries in the North Carolina economy is what led us to create Well Crafted NC, a documentation project focused on researching, preserving and providing access to materials related to the history of beer and brewing in North Carolina. We all work in the University Libraries at the University of North Carolina at Greensboro. Richard is

A pre–Triad Brewers Alliance label for a Triad-area brewery collaboration, 2015. *Gibb's Hundred Brewing Co.*

the digital technologies consultant, David is the digitization coordinator and Erin is the university archivist. We wanted to combine our professional knowledge and skills in partnership with the North Carolina craft beer community to record and make their history accessible.

Through historical research, oral history interviews with industry professionals and collecting records from modern craft breweries, Well Crafted NC seeks to tell the long history of how beer and brewing have affected North Carolina. We also work to preserve and provide access to the materials that help tell the ever-changing story of North Carolina craft beer today. All our oral history interviews, as well as many of the documents we have gathered from the generous people working in the North Carolina craft beer industry, can be found on our website: WellCraftedNC.com. This collection of resources documenting craft beer in North Carolina today is constantly growing.

The craft beer industry is one that changes quickly, and we knew that it would look different in ten years. Our Well Crafted NC project began with a focus on beer and brewing in Downtown Greensboro, and within months of starting the project, yet another new craft brewery had opened in the downtown business district. We soon realized, however, that focusing on Downtown Greensboro—or even on Greensboro as a whole—would not suffice. The craft beer community is so interconnected, with brewers moving from one brewery to another and collaborations on beers and events. Soon after finishing that initial phase of the project, we expanded our scope to focus on documenting the state of the industry throughout North Carolina.

In this book, we are pulling back that scope to focus solely on the Triad region, highlighting some of the stories and histories about beer and brewing in the Triad that we have found or recorded while working on Well Crafted NC. Defining what constitutes the "Piedmont Triad" region can be tricky. While the region is centered on three cities—Greensboro, High Point and Winston-Salem—the boundaries beyond those cities are less well defined. For this book, we have decided to adopt the geographical boundaries used by the Triad Brewers Alliance, a regional association for craft brewing professionals. The Triad Brewers Alliance includes eleven counties in its

Rebecca Spence of Haw River Farmhouse Ales in Saxapahaw is interviewed by the Well Crafted NC team for their ongoing documentation project. *Well Crafted NC.*

Tap handles and brews on display at Natty Greene's downtown Greensboro brewpub. *Natty Greene's Brewing Co.*

Hand-painted themed murals decorate the walls of the taproom at Fiddlin' Fish Brewing Co. in Winston-Salem. *Well Crafted NC.*

definition of the Triad. In addition to Guilford County (which includes Greensboro and High Point) and Forsyth County (which includes Winston-Salem), the Triad includes Alamance, Caswell, Davidson, Davie, Randolph, Rockingham, Stokes, Surrey and Yadkin Counties.

We start our history in the 1700s in the Moravian community of Bethabara, located in the current city of Winston-Salem. We will visit saloons and speakeasies. We will see how "big beer" companies like Miller and Schlitz affected the region with massive production facilities. We will wind through the decades until we get to 2020, a year of challenges for everyone, including the craft beer industry.

Along the way, you will meet people like Brother Heinrich Feldhausen, who was the brewer and distiller for the Bethabara community in 1750s until he was expelled because he "yielded to carnal desires and fell into all kinds of sin and shame." You will meet C.C. Shoffner, who opened numerous saloons up and down Greensboro's Elm Street (including one in a building that is now home to Little Brother Brewing). You will learn about Patricia Henry, a Bennett College graduate who became the first African American

Brewhouse operations at Gibb's Hundred Brewing's original site in downtown Greensboro. *Gibb's Hundred Brewing Co.*

Brewery taprooms have become important social "third spaces" across the Triad. Jasper enjoys the weather at Joymonger's Brewing Co. in Greensboro. *Well Crafted NC.*

woman brewmaster at a major brewery in the United States. Then after we explore some vital state and local legislative changes, we will learn about the people and businesses driving the region's craft brewing boom of the 2010s.

Ultimately, we hope you will see how integral beer history is to North Carolina history—and to American history in general. Beer history is American history, for better and for worse. Next time you crack open a can of Foothills Jade IPA or enjoy a Potters Clay Amber Ale from Four Saints or step into any of the dozens of brewery taprooms and brewpubs across the Triad region, maybe give a little toast to all the people across the centuries who have worked to make the Triad beer industry what it is today.

Prost!

BEER AND BREWING IN EARLY NORTH CAROLINA

Brewing in North Carolina began in the home, with women brewing batches of beer for consumption by their own families. As early as 1737, however, North Carolina's coastal counties were producing and exporting cider, persimmon beer, cedar beer, treacle beer and numerous spirits once described as "the pleasantest Drink I ever tasted, either in the Indies or Europe."[2] By 1770, multiple taverns and a commercial brewery were in operation in the town of Cross Creek, now Fayetteville.[3]

In 1753, the first Moravian settlers crossed the Yadkin River into what is now Forsyth County after initially settling in Georgia and Pennsylvania. The Moravians "came to transform the wilderness, not to be changed by it. Clearing a few acres to wrestle a little food from the ground was not enough. They wanted to build a community where they could protect their simple way of life, practice their religion with little interference, and live in godly, brotherly industry."[4]

Following settlements in Georgia and Pennsylvania, Count Ludwig von Zinzendorf, the Austrian leader of the sect, purchased nearly 100,000 acres of land along Muddy Creek that came to be known as Der Wachau, commemorating an Austrian estate owned by Zinzendorf's family. The name was later Latinized to Wachovia. The church took possession of the land from the Earl of Granville for £500 down and £150 in annual rent. To help finance the transaction, shares of 2,000 acres were sold, presumably to outsiders.[5]

BETHABARA

Bethabara (Hebrew for "House of Passage") was the initial Moravian settlement in the Wachovia area, with settlers arriving in 1753. By 1756, it consisted of sixty-five buildings and had become a commercial magnet for the surrounding area. Among these early buildings in the settlement were the first brewery and the first tavern, both of which began operation in 1756. Brother Heinrich Feldhausen was in charge of the brewery and distillery, and in the process, he became the first documented commercial brewer in what would be the Piedmont Triad region as well as the first in the colony of North Carolina. Brother Feldhausen was by all accounts well liked and good at his job; proceeds from the operation totaled £114 in 1759, which would have covered a significant part of the annual rent on the entire Wachovia tract. Bethabara was crushed when Feldhausen was expelled from the community in 1762 after he "yielded to carnal desires and fell into all kinds of sin and shame."[6]

The Moravians considered beer to have both nutritional and medicinal value, and they added a variety of herbs to the brew. Proscribed lunches for workers in 1758 included "if the work is very hard a little beer." Beer and spirits were sold both directly from the brewery and at the nearby tavern. Brethren Jacob Loesch and Erich Inglebretsen made the long trip to Salisbury in 1756 to secure a license for the tavern facility, which opened later that year.[7] By 1760, the tavern was operated by Brother Schaub and his wife, who promoted alfresco consumption by adding, in 1764, a "gallery in front of the entrance to the Tavern, so that the guests can stay outside more, especially in summer."[8]

Bethabara's economy was centralized and tightly controlled by the church. There was no private ownership of land, and individuals were licensed to operate specific businesses, such as the tavern and the brewery, but did not own them. The Shaubs handed over the reins to Brother and Sister Meyer in 1767, who were in charge until they made the move to Salem to run the tavern there, at which point the Shaubs took over again.[9]

By 1775, the original tavern building had been replaced with a new structure. Shortly after the relocation, the 1756 building collapsed, though it was well used during its short life.[10] Throughout its existence, the tavern was the site of major community gatherings, from funerals to traditional Moravian love feasts, which featured buns from the settlement's bakery and beer from the brewery. Located as it was in the only settled area for miles in any direction, the tavern was also popular with travelers and visitors from

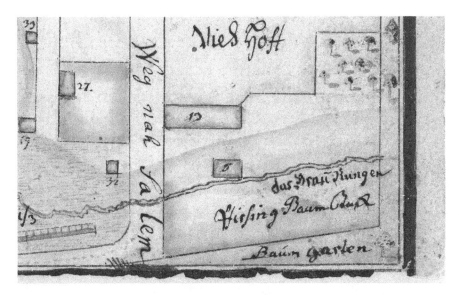

Detail of a map of Bethabara by Christian Gottlieb Reuter, with the brewery labeled no. 5 alongside the stream, 1766. The full image is available in the color insert. *Moravian Archives, Winston-Salem, NC.*

the hinterland, some of whom could be troublesome. Diaries of daily life in Bethabara record numerous instances of attempted forgery, fights and other nefarious acts. In fact, disturbances at the tavern were a big factor in the 1769 decision to appoint a constable for the settlement.[11] In 1767, the tavern was also a stop for no less a celebrity than Governor William Tryon, who enjoyed dinner at the tavern and a stop by the brewery afterward.[12]

The brewery and distillery itself had several different operators following Brother Feldhausen's ignominious departure, including his former apprentice Cristian Pfeiffer (1760s–1772), Peter Mücke (1772–1780s) and Phillip Vogler (1791). A new two-story (plus basement) "still-house" was constructed in 1777, but its fate was even more cruel than that of the original tavern. At about 5:30 p.m. on December 2, 1802, fire broke out in the distillery:

The house had been repaired recently, and in a few hours the large building was completely ruined, to our great sorrow. Those were anxious hours, which will never be forgotten by those who saw it. We believed that we had good reason to be sorely distressed, yet afterwards we saw that our tears should have been for gratitude instead of woe in view of the great danger which threatened our entire village and which was turned aside by the help and protection of the Saviour. No lives were lost, although it was difficult

The Herrman Buttner House at Bethabara, Winston-Salem, the rebuilt home of the Bethabara brewer and distiller. Completed on September 14, 1803. *Well Crafted NC.*

and dangerous to rescue some of the property; there could be no thought of putting out the fire, which spread rapidly through the building. When the fire broke out there was little wind, and that soon died away, which prevented danger to the rest of the village; and this was such an evidence of the gracious protection of God our Father and Saviour, that on the following day we felt impelled to bring to Him in unison the gratitude of our hearts, which took place in a public meeting, sorrowful yet with submission, and full of sympathy for the occupants of the house who had lost heavily by the fire. We besought the Saviour to be their comfort and their portion. We will remember thankfully the thought that was given to their great need both here and in other places.

This event caused much consideration of the distillery, both about the business and the rebuilding of the house. At a conference held here in Bethabara on the 12th, and at a meeting of the Aeltesten Conferenz on the 15th, it was resolved to make temporary arrangements for carrying on the distillery, and to rebuild the house.[13]

The distillery and brewery were indeed rebuilt. The following year, a new brewer's house—which still stands—was constructed on the site of the original distillery. Herrman Buttner was the first occupant of the new brewer's house, but he occupied it for only five years.[14] With the advent of Salem, brewing (and most other commerce) became less important in Bethabara. By 1805, the facility was operating at a loss, and the brewery's operations were reduced around 1807. Johann Christian Focke took over the operation at that point, but it seems to have closed for good by 1814.[15] The tavern closed in 1794 but reopened from 1801 to 1809. The tiny settlement was no longer the center of activity for Moravians (or for anyone else) in the area. Bethabara was doomed just thirteen years after its founding.

Salem

In 1766, the church established the town of Salem several miles to the southeast of Bethabara. The new town was an immediate success and grew quickly, drawing tradespeople and most Moravians away from the original settlement. Between 1766 and 1772, Bethabara's population dropped from about 130 to 54.[16] As in Bethabara, Salem's economy was closely controlled by the church. Tradespeople like Brother Winkler, the baker, were "privileged" with the right to engage in certain businesses free from competition. There was no private property, only a leasehold system in which it was possible to own only one's house and not the land on which it was built. Unmarried men lived communally in the large Single Brothers House where they also did their own baking and cooking.

As early as 1772, residents and leaders expressed their desire for a brewery in Salem, both to stem the consumption of stronger spirituous liquors and to build the economy, "for beer would be much more wholesome for our Brethren, and the neighbors would buy it in quantity."[17] The Single Brothers took on the task of providing beer and distilled beverages to the town in 1774, operating from a new building on Shallowford Street (now the south side of Academy Street between Marshall Street and Old Salem Road) just west of the center of town. The distillery produced rye, brandy, "peach spirits," peach brandy and cordial, among other things. One beer recipe instructs: "To 4 barrels of beer add about 1 tablespoon of ground coriander seed, putting it into the cooling vat, in order to give it a pleasant taste. To this

The Single Brothers' Brewery in Salem. This view of the brewery was taken from the northeast. *Old Salem Museums and Gardens.*

same quantity one may add a piece of rosin the size of a nut, boiling it with the beer. This gives the beer good color and body."[18]

The brewery and distillery were essential to Salem's economy. The Moravians also operated a busy tavern that opened in 1772.[19] While the brewery was a commercial operation that sold to "outsiders," the tavern, which burned down and was quickly rebuilt in 1784, also became a primary means of distribution. As in Bethabara, the tavern could be controversial at times, and the sale of alcohol became more and more directed toward travelers and visitors from outside Salem. In 1805, the brewery and distillery operation was discontinued with the idea of turning the site into a farm. Production apparently resumed for a few more years starting with the 1812 arrival of David and Sara Blum, who migrated to Salem from Bethabara to take over the brewery and tavern. Blum stressed that visitors should not be served too much alcohol and "locals" should not be served any.[20]

By 1803, it had already been proposed "that no strong drink shall be dispensed in the Tavern on Sunday, except to travelers" and noted that this was "entirely according to the wish of the Conferenz."[21] By 1850, the tavern had been sold to Adam Butner, under a leasehold, as the economy of the village became less centralized. There were continuing concerns about drunkenness in the taverns and inn, and Moravians could no longer be served there at all by 1852.

Salem Tavern, located in Old Salem, 1784. *Well Crafted NC.*

The tavern, however, was not the only retail outlet for beer in Salem. Brother Winkler provided beer and spirits along with baked goods. Dissatisfaction with his operations led to the end of his monopoly in 1837, when James Hall was given permission to open a competing bakery, which would also sell beer (but no other alcoholic beverages). By 1850, the tavern was being operated as a summer resort and had become known as "the hotel." It closed sometime in the late 1880s.[22]

Salem Meets Winston

In 1848, the last of several divisions of Stokes County resulted in the creation of Forsyth County, which would contain both Bethabara and Salem. The new county needed a seat, and Salem adamantly refused the honor. The Moravians then sold fifty-four acres immediately north of Salem for a town that became Winston, the new county seat, in 1851.

From the beginning, the two towns had a close relationship. Winston's "open" economy was not bound by the rules of the church and complemented the older settlement, which ultimately became something of a bedroom community for the commercial center in Winston. Winston became home to hotels, stores and saloons (as will be discussed in the next chapter) and was apparently a fairly rough place compared to the staid and upright Moravian town to the south. By the end of the nineteenth century, the two towns shared a post office and were generally thought of as one entity. In 1913, the marriage became official. Winton and Salem merged into the new city of Winston-Salem, the most populous city in the state in 1920.

Winston-Salem also shared a kinship with the neighboring cities of Greensboro and High Point as well as the largely rural hinterland. The region that would eventually become known as the "Piedmont Triad" shared many things, but to say there was a common view toward the sale and consumption of alcohol throughout the region would be extremely misleading. Despite Forsyth County's early leadership in both brewing and distilling, the trades were not universally accepted, even by the Moravians, and the more conservative Scotch-Irish in neighboring cities often held somewhat different views than their German brethren in the Twin City.

2

SALOONS OF THE TRIAD

The Triad was home to numerous purveyors of beer and spirits during the 1800s. From the taverns that catered to weary travelers with food, drink and accommodations to the saloons with their more limited scope, it was not hard to find a drink, particularly in Guilford and Forsyth Counties. The original Moravian taverns in Salem and Bethabara were less important to the trade than they had been in the previous century, while saloons became a very visible part of street life first in Greensboro and later in the new town of Winston. In the less urbanized areas, from Mocksville to Kernersville to King, taverns catered to travelers as well as locals.

It is sometimes difficult to distinguish between a saloon, a store and a restaurant during the nineteenth century, so on some level, it may be safest to group all the purveyors mentioned in this chapter under the general category of "retailers" since there were some aspects of each subcategory in most. Saloons sold beer and spirits for home consumption, restaurants were often either adjacent to or included on-premises saloons and wholesalers were also likely to own a significant proportion of the retail outlets.

The Saloon Scene in Greensboro

Greensborough was established in 1808 as a new seat for Guilford County, one that was more centrally located than Martinsville, the site of the 1781

Battle of Guilford Courthouse. Lacking navigable water transportation, Greensborough remained a relatively sleepy place until the years after the Civil War, when transportation and manufacturing transformed the town into something resembling a city, with a modernized and simplified spelling of its name adding to the package in 1895. The city's significant railroad infrastructure spurred a considerable hospitality industry as the century closed, meaning new hotels, new eating houses and new saloons. By 1900, the population exceeded ten thousand, and Greensboro was home to at least nine saloons, along with five hotels and fourteen restaurants.

Again, distinctions between types of businesses could often be somewhat blurry in the 1800s. Most hotels had saloons attached, as did some restaurants. Additionally, by the mid-1890s, several "oyster saloons" around Greensboro sold alcohol, cheap food and cigars. B.Y. Dean opened the Dean and Bugbee Billiard Saloon in Greensboro's Garrett Block in 1868 (near the north side of West Market Street, between Elm and Greene Streets). In 1870, his oyster saloon was described in the *Greensboro Patriot* as "one of the coziest little places in town" and inspired a pun suggesting that patrons "who are *stew*-diously inclined will find all they want there."[23]

A view of the Hotel Clegg (*left*) and R.P. Gorrell Saloon (*right*) on Elm Street in Greensboro, 1896. Note the proximity of the railroad tracks. *Greensboro History Museum.*

Elisha Giles Newcomb was one of many who straddled the line between the retail and wholesale trades. Born in Virginia in 1848, the Confederate army veteran and former prisoner of war moved to Greensboro in 1872 and married his wife, Emma, a year later.[24] That same year, he opened a book and stationery store that also featured a "news depot," though by 1875 he had become a grocery salesman in the employ of Seymour Steele, who later operated Greensboro's Central Hotel.[25] From this, Newcomb went on to manage the McAdoo House hotel and, in 1880, the Central Hotel. The McAdoo opened in 1874 at Elm and Washington Streets and was one of Greensboro's best-known hotels for years. By 1883, advertisements place Newcomb back at the McAdoo House, this time as a purveyor of beer, wine and spirits, although by 1890, Herman Lohman had charge of the hotel bar. The McAdoo operated until it was destroyed by a major fire in May 1916.[26]

Newcomb's retail and wholesale business relocated to the Odell Hardware building at 327 South Elm Street by 1887. Presumably, he operated a saloon on both premises; by the time he moved a block north to 231 South Elm, there was definitely a saloon in the mix. It is this location that the *Reidsville Review* praised as "one of the handsomest bars in the Piedmont section":

No matter how widely we may differ as to the right of drinking alcoholic stimulants, there are two points upon which every sane man will agree, "viz;" that the city by virtue of its license, grants the licensee the privilege to sell, and makes his business as lawful as any other, with the same right of protection by the law as any other line of merchandise. Secondly, if one must drink, he should drink at places where the purest goods are handled. His place is fitted up luxuriously and is the Bon-Ton saloon of the city as well as of the Piedmont section.

Mr. Newcomb has beyond a question the most select stock of Kentucky and Pennsylvania whiskey as well as imported wines, beers, ales and cordials to be found in North Carolina. The finest line of both domestic and foreign cigars is also in stock.

Mr. Newcomb is a native of Virginia and is an educated and polite gentleman. One can drink at his place without having his ears filled with profane language or be brought in contact with occurrences of a demoralizing and disreputable character. He runs a saloon, not a grog shop and everything in his place is in strict accordance with law, not only of the land, but of common sense and good taste. He is one of the oldest whiskey men in the

State and has ever been a representative one. It would never be any trouble to get license in any place, if all saloon men ran their places upon the high principles that Mr. Newcomb conducts his business.[27]

When the dispensary law forced the closure of all Greensboro saloons in 1899, Newcomb refused to shut down and was arrested for retailing liquor in violation of the law.[28] He was, however, granted a license to open a saloon after the system was dismantled in Greensboro in 1901. Prohibition proved too much for "Major Newcomb," and he retreated to Petersburg, Virginia, staying there until his death in 1915.[29]

Down Elm Street toward the railroad tracks, Greensboro had even more saloons in the area that came to be known as "Hamburger Square" due to all its cheap eating and drinking establishments. Proximity to the railroad tracks meant that the area had a somewhat transient population that could be housed in the many small hotels in the area. The railroad tracks also made the 300 and 400 blocks of South Elm Street a convenient spot for wholesalers and distributors as well as retailers. The Robert Portman Brewing Company had its local depot right by the train station close to the present-day intersection of Smothers Place and Spring Garden Street.[30]

One saloon operator in this part of Greensboro was Samuel Johnson McCauley. Born in Orange County, North Carolina, in 1847, McCauley

The Hotel Clegg in downtown Greensboro, circa 1906. Both Samuel McCauley and Charles C. Shoffner ran saloons within the hotel. *From* Commercial History of the State of North Carolina.

McCauley's Saloon, popularly known as "The Cascade Saloon," in the left foreground nestled between two rail lines, circa 1900. *Greensboro History Museum.*

served in the Confederate army during the Civil War, enlisting at age seventeen.[31] By 1885, McCauley held a liquor license in Greensboro. His first saloon, which like most saloons also offered items for offsite consumption, was in a wooden building at 408 South Elm Street with railroad tracks on both sides. Following an 1891 explosion and fire that threatened the wooden building, it was reinforced with an outer brick shell in 1895, though business was apparently never interrupted by the construction.[32] News articles about McCauley's, several of them including racially tinged descriptions of fights, suggest that it was integrated and often patronized by Black Greensboro residents and visitors.[33] McCauley sold this saloon in 1901, moving his operations to the saloon at the nearby Hotel Clegg.

By 1906, once saloons were banned in Greensboro, the space that held McCauley's first saloon was occupied by an eating house operated by Wiley Weaver. Weaver was a Black business owner operating on the main street in town, which was unusual in the South at that time.[34] Over the next century, the building housed a number of restaurants, wholesale grocers, storage warehouses and other businesses. Historically, it has become known as the Cascade Saloon, though it is unclear when it took that name. Although photographs dating to at least 1903 show the name painted on the building's façade, the only occupant listed in city directories using the word *cascade* was a pool hall that operated from about 1913 to 1926. After years of neglect and threats of demolition, the building was restored for use as the local headquarters of the Christman Company in 2018.[35]

Another prominent Greensboro saloon owner was Charles C. Shoffner. Shoffner was born on a farm in Alamance County in 1868. By 1898, he was working as a salesman for the Richardson Drug Company in Greensboro (later Richardson-Vicks) and filed an application for a liquor license in Greensboro. His saloon was in the Jones and Taylor Building at 346 South Elm Street, now the site of Little Brother Brewing.[36] The Greensboro saloon remained open until the first dispensary law forced its closure the

The Cascade Saloon on South Elm Street in downtown Greensboro before renovations began in 2017. *The Christman Company.*

The view down South Elm Street in Greensboro, featuring the J.R. Stewart Saloon in the left foreground, circa 1904. *Greensboro History Museum.*

following year, but it was also one of the first to reopen in 1901.[37] In the interim, Shoffner moved to Winston and listed his occupation for the census as a liquor dealer.

By 1902, Shoffner was operating saloons in both Greensboro and Winston. He split with his Greensboro partner, J.R. Stewart, and migrated to a new location in Greensboro's Clegg Hotel in 1902.[38] Stewart retained the saloon at 346 South Elm. In Winston, Shoffner partnered with George Roediger, from whom he purchased his saloon building outright in 1906, following the final closure of all saloons in Greensboro.[39]

THE SALOON SCENE IN WINSTON AND SALEM

After Winston was established as the commercial counterpart to Salem, it fulfilled its destiny quite well. The twin cities grew from a population of 443 in 1880 to over 13,000 in 1900, and the diversified manufacturing enterprises in the city, led by tobacco and textiles, had produced a booming economy. While Winston-Salem would have a complicated relationship with regulation of alcoholic beverages (not unlike the Moravian Church that had given birth to the region), there would be a steady string of saloons in Winston until statewide prohibition came.

Like Greensboro's Hamburger Square, Winston developed an identifiable nucleus of saloons and eating houses in the vicinity of Third and Main Streets in the 1890s. C.A. Winkler's lager beer saloon, licensed in 1879, was located on Main near Third as of 1882. Chap Bodenheimer opened the Up-to-Date Saloon at 9 East Third Street, near the corner of Main, sometime before 1903. Bodenheimer and H.R. Douthit, his partner, operated the saloon until the beginning of national Prohibition, when it was replaced by a restaurant.[40]

Nearby, Samuel Shermer and Josiah Phillips had a relatively uneventful ten-year run at 218–220 East Second Street from 1896 to 1906, making their establishment one of the longer-lived saloons in town at the time. From 1896 to about 1903, they also had a second location nearby at 138 Depot Street (Now North Patterson Avenue).[41] The only "newsworthy" incident for the partners seems to have happened in 1905, when their employee J.W. Warren had what was called a "peculiar" accident:

While tapping a keg of beer the wooden stopper flew out, striking him on the nose and knocking him down. Mr. Warren was unconscious for an hour or more. The accident was caused by an accumulation of gas in the keg, which, after the stopper being loosened, came in contact with air and exploded.[42]

Hotels were also popular sites for saloons in Winston. In 1882, Messrs. Alsop and Bush opened a beer saloon in the basement of the four-year-old Central Hotel near Second and Main. The saloon offered billiards, pool and bathing rooms. Winston's famed Hotel Zinzendorf opened in West End in 1891 and burned to the ground less than two years later. The Zinzendorf was reborn in 1906 in a more central location on Main Street between Second and Third, replacing the old Hotel Jones. The new hostelry, considered one of the finest in the state, had a well-regarded saloon. This caused some problems in the saloon district just north; the sentiment of some members of the Board of Aldermen was that no new saloons should be licensed on the south side of Third Street because of proximity to the new hotel. Several licenses were not renewed, and some saloons consolidated operations across the street.

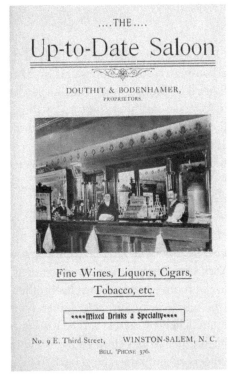

Right: Douthit and Bodenhamer's Up-To-Date Saloon at No. 9 East Third Street in Winston. *From* Walsh's Directory of the Cities of Winston and Salem, N.C. for 1902 and 1903.

Below: Interior, Theodore K. Renigar's Saloon, located at 12 East Third Street in Winston, circa 1905. *Old Salem Museums and Gardens.*

The Kobres: A Family Affair

Occupying the space at 14–16 East Third Street in 1902 was a saloon and adjoining restaurant operated by Max Kobre and his brothers Henry and Sam. The Kobres were Russian Jewish immigrants who apparently arrived in Winston just after the turn of the century; the brothers do not appear in the 1900 census and are first mentioned in print resources in Winston in 1902. Aside from minor infractions common to most such enterprises at the time, such as keeping the bar and restaurant open later than the mandatory 8:00 p.m. closing time, their first few years in America seem to have been relatively uneventful.

That would change on the night of January 21, 1906, a Sunday, when Henry Kobre was murdered in the room he shared with Sam, launching an investigation and trial that would be covered in newspapers as far away as New York City. After work on Sunday night, twenty-year-old Sam Kobre returned to the room he shared with his brother Henry and was startled to find Henry, who was wearing his nightclothes, lying on the floor in a pool of blood. Sam immediately ran across to the Hotel Phoenix at Fourth and Liberty and phoned his brother Max before going to the police station to report the crime. Two officers accompanied Sam back to the room, where Henry was placed on the bed to await transport to Twin-City Hospital. Fifteen minutes after arriving at the hospital, Henry was pronounced dead. He never regained consciousness.[43] Later that night, a bullet was recovered from the ceiling of the room. Sam Kobre suspected robbery, noting that his brother always carried a substantial amount of cash in his purse, none of which was found at the scene. There was also evidence that someone had broken into the saloon through the back door. No bullet was found in the body by the corner.[44]

In early February, Max Kobre, along with the City of Winston, the State of North Carolina, the *Winston-Salem Journal* and several individuals (many of them fellow saloonkeepers) established a reward fund for information about the murder. Things took a rather odd turn on the night of February 15 when a medium by the name of Kitty Baldwin, holding a seance in Greensboro, was asked about the murder. Baldwin apparently "began to describe a man going into a saloon with two men following him. Then suddenly she began to shriek that there was a hole in his head and rushed frantically from her chair. The occurrence created a small sensation."[45] This was not the last instance of a paranormal connection to the case.

On Monday, March 5, 1906, Sam Kobre and William Plean, a retail clerk in the store of A. Shapiro, were arrested for the robbery and murder of

Henry Kobre. Plean was arrested on his return to Winston following his wedding. Sam Kobre was arrested while attending a play at the Elks Club. A tip from sixteen-year-old Sallie Stewart led to both arrests. Stewart claimed to have been intimately involved with Sam, though the *Winston-Salem Journal* questioned her credibility based on her status as a "scarlet woman" and her arrest for "creating a nuisance." Henry Kobre was said to have been carrying anywhere from $1,200 to $1,700 at the time of the murder. The fact that Plean and Henry Kobre had visited Emiline Gardner, a fortune-teller in Salem, to inquire about their fate was cited as evidence of their guilt. Later testimony showed that the defendants had visited not one but *two* fortune-tellers, one white and one Black. J.E. Whitbeck, manager of the Portner Brewing Company depot in Winston, was also implicated as the "mastermind," both by Stewart and another unnamed witness. A fourth suspect, a transient nicknamed "Finger," was also named but never identified or charged.[46]

The trial began on Tuesday, May 29, 1906. Sallie Stewart testified to the involvement of Sam Kobre, William Plean, J.E. Whitbeck and "Finger." Stewart stated that a planned and coordinated attack was carried out by the four in which Henry Kobre was brutally beaten and robbed. Others, however, testified that Kobre and Plean had been at Max Kobre's house playing cards until after 11:00 p.m., leaving no time for them to be involved in such an attack. Police officers and a streetcar conductor corroborated the timeline. Whitbeck testified that he had been nowhere near the scene and that, contrary to her assertions, he did not know Sallie Stewart. Numerous saloon owners, including Cicero Orrell and T.K. Renigar, testified at the trial as well.[47]

The brief trial ended in acquittal on Thursday, May 31. Judge Peebles sent the jury to deliberate with the instruction that they find the defendants not guilty. Otherwise, he stated, he would set the verdict aside. "I couldn't let a yellow dog be hanged on her testimony," he said of Sallie Stewart, noting that none of her testimony had been corroborated and that she had even contradicted herself on several occasions. The judge's theory was that Henry Kobre probably heard someone trying to break in and was shot when he looked out the window, resulting in the odd position that had been noted earlier. No further mention was made of the missing money.[48]

Max Kobre's saloon license was not renewed after 1906. In 1908, he applied for a "near beer" license, but by 1910, he had relocated to Baltimore and then to Danville, Virginia, hometown of his wife.[49] He eventually returned to Baltimore and died there in 1952. Sam Kobre also relocated to Danville, where he was apparently involved in some questionable business deals and took his own life in 1933.[50] The upper floor of Kobre's saloon—presumably including the "murder room"—was converted into a motion picture theater for Black audiences in 1909.[51]

The Saloon Scene in Other Parts of the Triad

Rockingham County experienced something of a saloon boom in 1906, following Greensboro's "dry" vote.[52] W.J. Lewis of Walnut Cove owned Wood's Up-to-Date Saloon in Madison in that year, but the name suggests an earlier history, presumably connected to a Mr. Wood. The establishment included a restaurant that served "nice, regular meals" for a quarter and lunches that ranged from ten to twenty cents.[53]

Reidsville had numerous saloons, which seem to have centered on the area of Southwest Market Street by the railroad tracks. By 1889, William Young had opened the Opera House Saloon for what was a fairly long run, providing oysters as well as beer and spirits. Davie County corn whiskey

Patrons pose with a dog in a Reidsville saloon. *Left to right*: Ike Sharp, Mr. Gillie (owner), Charlie Thomas, Babe Hooper and Bob Parrish. *Rockingham Community College Foundation, Inc., Historical Collections, Gerald B. James Library.*

was "a specialty."[54] Young later operated the City Saloon at West Market and Morehead (which was taken over by B.F. Sprinkle, an associate, in 1897 and renamed the City Bar).[55] By 1901, Young was operating Young's Saloon in the Lehman Building with B.F. Sprinkle as one of his bartenders.[56] Wood Small had operated a saloon on Gilmer Street, which he sold to W.W. Vernon in 1891; Small then opened the Bonanza Saloon on West Market Street.[57] H.C. Sheets, a distiller from Danbury, opened a retail outlet for his output in 1906.[58]

High Point and Lexington were, for the most part, officially dry in the years before Prohibition, as was most of Alamance County, though Graham did ultimately opt for a dispensary.

3

PROHIBITION IN THE TRIAD

North Carolina has a long history of legislative attempts to control both the consumption of alcohol in the state and who consumes it, stretching back to before independence. As early as 1715, the General Assembly passed a law attempting to not only address public drunkenness and disorderly conduct but also regulate liquor sales through container size, commodity pricing and government licensure.[59]

By the early 1820s, the temperance movement in North Carolina was well underway. One of the earliest organized temperance societies in the state, if not the first, was founded in Guilford County in May 1822 and encouraged others to use their influence to create similar, like-minded societies in the Triad.[60] They were followed in the early to mid-1800s by such organizations as the North Carolina Temperance Society in 1839; the Washingtonians, a precursor to Alcoholics Anonymous, in 1841; and the Sons of Temperance in 1843. These movements were focused on encouraging individuals to avoid alcohol, not necessarily on influencing public policy and business operation.

The temperance movement, however, did not mean that alcohol consumption was low. North Carolina's tendency to "vote dry and drink wet" was much lampooned in the local press. The *People's Press* in Winston quipped in 1855, "One of our Western villages passed an ordinance forbidding taverns to sell liquor on the Sabbath to any person except travelers. The next Sunday every other man in town was seen walking around with a valise in one hand and two saddle-bags in the other."[61]

Winston and Salem were the closest urban area to the "drier" counties of Western North Carolina and, as such, served as a major retail source for beer, wine and spirits for the western counties. Even so, residents were conflicted about just how much of this business there should be. As was the case for most businesses, the laissez-faire environment in Winston proved much more friendly to the free operation of alcohol retailing than did the tightly controlled Moravian economy in Salem, even as that economy became less centralized. Winston was not "wide open" by any standard, however, and attempts to regulate or even prohibit the sale of alcoholic beverages started almost immediately after its founding.

Three years after Winston's establishment in 1866, the Board of Aldermen essentially prohibited the retailing of liquor by anyone who had been unlicensed to do so before the founding of the town by saying that no further licenses would be issued.[62] This position was reinforced in 1870 when the prohibition of retail liquor sales and bowling within the town limits was made official, apparently to some extent as a reaction to B.Y. Dean's application for a saloon and bowling alley that same year. By 1877, however, sentiment had become more liberal—at least with respect to lager beer and ale—as the Board of Alderman determined that a $500 license fee provided a sufficient remedy to any ill effects that such sales might produce. In 1879, a new town charter permitted the taxing of liquor and beer sales as well as gambling, effectively legalizing all the assorted vices. The first "lager beer saloon" license was granted to Salem baker and confectioner C.A. Winkler in 1879, and the first "new" liquor license was issued to J.F. Ward in 1882. Several others followed shortly thereafter. Despite an 1886 referendum indicating public support for some level of prohibition, alcohol sales continued in Winston.[63]

Temperance sentiment was a bit more aggressive in Greensboro. On May 1, 1876, Morehead and Gilmer Township (Greensboro straddles the two) voted themselves "dry." The initial vote potentially exempted beer and wine, but that was quickly overturned, making all intoxicating beverages illegal in Greensboro and the surrounding area. One local saloonkeeper apparently draped his premises in mourning cloth after the vote.[64] Thomas King moved his saloon and "wet groceries" establishment to Brown's Summit, just outside the reach of the ordinance, offering "the lovers of GOOD WHISKY, BRANDY, WINE, BEER, etc." to "any and everybody wanting something nice to drink."[65] The Greensboro temperance experiment failed and was repealed two years later.

The invention of artificial refrigeration, year-round brewing, greater access to cold-brewed lagers and the transport of alcoholic beverages a greater distance away from the brewery itself without spoilage brought a growth in the number of saloons. For example, Winston almost doubled the number of saloons between 1884 and 1890 from six to ten. This expansion of the brewing industry, and particularly the number of saloons, started to bend the personal temperance movement into an anti-saloon crusade. This new version of the movement created a shift in focus from the betterment of society through personal abstinence to prohibition through legislation and legal enforcement.

Temperance Organizations

By 1880, the number of temperance societies in the state were growing, especially in the Triad. The most prominent of these groups was the Woman's Christian Temperance Union (WCTU), a national organization founded in 1874 that advocated for a broad platform of social and legislative change. In addition to Prohibition, the WCTU was active in the fight for equal rights and women's suffrage as well as pushing for the legislative control of narcotics, prostitution and gambling, among many other causes.

The North Carolina chapter of the WCTU was founded in May 1881 with Mary Jarvis, wife of Governor Thomas Jordan Jarvis, as president.[66] A local Greensboro union followed soon after, forming on April 3, 1883. By August, the Greensboro union had grown to seventy active members.[67] All three publications related to the Woman's Christian Temperance Union in the state were based in the Triad. *Woman's Temperance Advocate* was published in 1884 in Greensboro by Thomas, Reece & Co. *Anchor* (1885) and *North Carolina White Ribbon* (1896) were published directly by the WCTU of North Carolina, with *Anchor* produced in Greensboro and *North Carolina White Ribbon* printed first in High Point and then in Greensboro.

Two other organizations founded in the Triad during this period include a local chapter of the national Prohibition Party and the Temperance Reform Club. The Temperance Reform Club was local to Winston, and its autumn 1887 meeting purportedly included four hundred attendees, all male.[68] A committee to organize a North Carolina chapter of the national Prohibition Party of the United States first met in Randolph County in 1884. On December 10, 1885, a group of eighty delegates met in Greensboro and adopted a resolution 76–4 to formally organize the party in North Carolina with "the Prohibition of the Liquor Traffic its

"Under Prohibition" political cartoon by Winsor McCay detailing the ills of Prohibition, from high crime to highball parties. *From the* Greensboro Record, *April 17, 1927.*

prime object"[69] and to have a slate of candidates in the 1886 and 1888 elections. The members would appear to have had little to no effect on the elections, though their focus on political advocacy and legislative change was a harbinger of things to come.

ALCOHOL ON THE BALLOT

The North Carolina General Assembly authorized the first statewide voter referendum on prohibition in 1881.[70] If passed, the law would have made the manufacture, purchase or sale of alcohol a misdemeanor, except for a few loopholes such as for medicinal use. This would have required a pharmacy prescription, and then no more than a gallon could be given out at a time. When the election was held in August 1881, the measure was soundly defeated 166,325 to 48,370, and not a single county in the Triad voted in favor of prohibition.[71]

On February 16, 1899, after its first attempt at prohibition ended after two years, Greensboro opted for another experiment in temperance, voting to adopt the dispensary system by a staggering 531–2.[72] The dispensary system essentially moved all retail sales of alcoholic beverages to one state-chartered store, mandating the closure of all saloons and other retailers—or at least forcing them into other lines of business. In Greensboro, the dispensary was in the space that had housed C.C. Shoffner's saloon at 346 South Elm Street, and Jonathan McCauley, a bartender at McCauley's saloon, was hired as clerk.[73]

The dispensary system was something less than a success in Greensboro. Though revenues to the county increased, there was controversy almost from opening day. Within the first month of its operation, the dispensary's manager, clerk and porter had all been charged with selling whiskey to a minor.[74] The manager, Captain Briscoe B. Bouldin, resigned in early August, apparently over a salary dispute.[75] McCauley, the clerk and interim manager, resigned about a week later, and stated that he had been "hired to quit" and was receiving "the same amount of pay to walk the streets that he got as dispensary clerk."[76] The dispensary system's constitutionality was challenged (and upheld) before the North Carolina Supreme Court on the argument that the city did not have the required authority.[77]

By the summer of 1900, Greensboro had had enough. Amid support for the dispensary from the city fathers and the press—and an ugly race-based appeal that mandated only white voters should be permitted to weigh in on the question—a referendum was held on August 2, 1900.[78] Greensboro opted out of the dispensary system with a majority of over seventy-one votes. According to the *Greensboro Telegram*, "No one took the trouble to attempt to find out just the number of ballots that sealed the fate of the dispensary. Everyone knew that it was sufficient and was satisfied."[79] Winston never initiated the dispensary system at all.

By 1899, it was becoming apparent that local option laws were not working as anticipated. There were ongoing reversals in both dispensary and local option laws every two years, which brought about confusion and instability, while wet and dry advocates assailed one another in the newspapers and politically. The local option laws increased the amount of bootlegging going on in the state, an operation largely concentrated in the Piedmont Triad area, to the point where between 1877 and 1881 there were 4,061 stills seized and 7,339 alcohol-related arrests, while 26 officers were killed and 57 wounded in while enforcing dry laws.[80] Additionally, a "valise trade" in which people would simply travel to the areas where alcohol was legal to purchase their drinks before returning to "dry" towns had been established. The *Greensboro Daily News* wrote about such a practice along the Southern Railway in 1906, when Greensboro had (again) voted itself dry while nearby Reidsville remained "wet:"

Almost each of the Southern's trains brings in a number of white and colored men every day for a supply of spirits. They alight from the train with several valises, telescopes, etc., and make a straight shoot for the saloons. It is always noticeable that these valises and telescopes are loaded down on the return trip. Saloons here are not allowed to shop whiskey to points in North Carolina, but they do a tremendous trade in the manner aforesaid....As the saloon tax in Reidsville is so exceedingly high, it is presumed that local saloon keepers depend to a great extent upon the amount of intoxicants they sell in the Gate City.[81]

As the 1800s gave way to the twentieth century, the legislative movement toward statewide prohibition gained momentum quickly. With the arrival of the North Carolina Anti-Saloon League in 1902, dry advocates had a well-funded and politically connected organization to not only push their prohibition platform through the General Assembly but also promote it to the populace at large. The North Carolina Anti-Saloon League was initially brought together by several religious organizations and chaired by former U.S. senator and Warrenton native J.W. Bailey. In many ways, the Anti-Saloon League could be called one of the first modern lobbying groups. Members were dedicated to legislative change and hyper-focused on a single issue, and they used this issue as a wedge with which to define candidates for elected office.

The league quickly began pushing for more anti-alcohol local option laws, but it also became a major force in passing two statewide laws on the path to Prohibition. The first of these was the Watts Act of 1903, which, in a targeted attack on rural distilleries, prohibited the manufacture or sale of spirits except in incorporated towns.[82] There were exceptions for wine, cider and alcohol with a prescription. The 1905 Ward Law followed, banning alcohol production in towns with fewer than one thousand residents.[83] By December 1908, only eighty towns in the state remained wet.[84]

In July 1907, famous hatchet-wielding Kansas prohibitionist Carrie Nation held a train tour across North Carolina. She praised Hickory for its passing of a local option law but noted that there were "sneaks around here who were hauling the accursed stuff around in their buggies and selling it."[85] On the other hand, Nation had very little polite to say about Salisbury, which she described as "a hell hole....You have plenty of saloons and every one of them is a ticket office to hell."[86] She also visited Greensboro twice, in response to which the *Greensboro Patriot* reported that "so far as we can judge, the cause of temperance has not been materially stimulated by her sojourn of a week or more in the state."[87]

In January 1907, the Anti-Saloon League formally adopted a platform endorsing statewide prohibition. One year later, Governor Robert B. Glenn called a special session of the General Assembly. Only one item was on the agenda—creating a statewide referendum on prohibition. Should it be approved by voters, the law[88] would go into effect in January the following year.

The statewide referendum was held on May 26, 1908. North Carolina became the third southern state to implement statewide prohibition and the first in the country to adopt prohibition by a direct vote of the people[89] when prohibition carried the day by a vote of 113,612 to 69,416.[90] In the Triad, Guilford, Forsyth and Randolph Counties all supported the dry cause with majorities of over 1,500 votes while Caswell, Stokes, Surrey and Yadkin Counties were the only Triad counties to go majority wet.[91]

IMPLEMENTING PROHIBITION IN THE TRIAD

As Prohibition laws in North Carolina continued to tighten and close loopholes, speakeasies (also called blind tigers and flying pigs) began to appear. Many former social clubs were easily converted into blind tigers, and the prohibition of "near beer" with less than a half of a percent of alcohol drove even more people to get their alcohol illegally. In the Triad, two blind tigers in Winston were busted the first week of January 1909.[92] By the end of 1909, a police officer told the *Winston-Salem Journal* that for every blind tiger disrupted, two more popped up.[93] By 1910, blind tigers in the city of High Point were said to be doing a "rushing business,"[94] and in Lexington, jugs of liquor were apparently being sold in broad daylight off Main Street. As a Lexington resident noted in a (spelling challenged) letter to the local paper that was reprinted in the *Greensboro Patriot*:

> *Before prohibition became effective in this state, citizens of Lexington had to go to the trouble of either going or sending to Salizbury [sic] for their "booze," but since we have a prohibition law, liquor is hauled into town in broad, open daytime and sold by the jugfull in less than one hundred yards from Main Street, almost as publicly as farmers sell sweet cider. There is such strong competition among the blind tigers of the two that bling [sic] tigering has become a poor business. The town is surrounded by four alleged near-beer saloons, no one of which could pay the tax and run thirty days if they sold nothing but near-beer, because near-beer is slop and not fit for a hog to drink.[95]*

Though the Triad did not see the organized crime violence of many larger cities like Chicago or New York, the bootlegging trade and blind tiger operations many times led to violence. Everett Hamilton was an African American detective in Greensboro who reported on Black-operated blind tigers in his community. Paid three dollars per conviction,[96] on a single day he was responsible for no fewer than twelve convictions in Greensboro.[97] One day in June 1910, Hamilton noticed several men loitering around his home on Whittington Street whom he believed to be Sapp Hogan, Tom Watson, Dave Whitfield and George Caldwell. All were men who ran blind tigers, and all at one point were turned in to police by Hamilton.[98] That night, Hamilton started receiving threatening phone calls, and the following evening his house was blown up by a dynamite bomb. The detective and his family escaped unharmed.[99]

By 1913, multiple laws supported by the Anti-Saloon League were passed in an attempt to curb blind tigers, to no apparent avail. In 1918, over 1,500 stills were found and destroyed in North Carolina.[100] In January of the following year, the North Carolina Senate ratified the Volstead Act unanimously, and the House followed suit 93–10, making North Carolina

Bootlegging bust near High Point in 1927. Note the man second from right holding a gun on three prisoners, circled. *P.M. Candle Moonshine Photographs and Letter #P0079, North Carolina Collection Photographic Archives, The Wilson Library, University of North Carolina at Chapel Hill.*

the eighth state to ratify the Eighteenth Amendment to the Constitution.[101] The General Assembly followed this up in 1923 with the Turlington Act, intended to bring the 1908 state prohibition law into conformity with the Eighteenth Amendment.[102]

Enforcement of both the Volstead and Turlington Acts proved problematic. Federal agents led by J.L. Osteen of Selica, North Carolina, were underfunded and undermanned, and there was no centralized state enforcement, with North Carolina relying on the county sheriff's offices with predictably variable results. Courts became overwhelmed with Prohibition-related cases, and in 1929 in the Triad alone there were 706 Prohibition criminal cases in court, compared to 772 total criminal cases.[103] That same year, Triad sheriffs and federal agents uncovered 1,998 distilleries, over 100 gallons of beer and 1,611,083 gallons of mash.[104] This rising trend continued into the 1930s, with 2,000 gallons of beer and 30 gallons of whiskey mash seized on the banks of the Catawba River in a bust in 1931[105] and the Guilford County sheriff seizing 538 gallons of whiskey and 320 gallons of beer in a single raid in 1932.[106] In a scene from a movie, seventeen-year-old Mackalina Rebecca Johnston led Prohibition agents on a four-and-a-half-mile chase from Wilkesboro to Moravian Falls with 50 gallons of whiskey in the back of her roadster.[107]

Despite the strain on the legal system and numerous questions as to the success or failure of the Prohibition effort, it appeared that North Carolina was to be solidly dry for the foreseeable future. That began to change with the stock market crash of 1929 and the onset of the Great Depression, and Prohibition quickly became as much an economic issue as a moral debate. By 1932, legal alcohol, especially beer with its lower alcohol by volume (ABV), was seen by many as a way to hasten depression recovery, lessen a growing crime rate and reduce unemployment.[108] In January 1933, the General Assembly passed a law legalizing the sale of beer, wine and fruit juices containing up to 3.2% alcohol.[109] As the law was put forth as economic recovery legislation, to refill treasury coffers there was a two-dollar tax per barrel and two-cent tax per twelve-ounce bottle placed per sale. Additional license fees of twenty-five dollars (county) and ten dollars (municipal) were tacked on as well. While the law did provide additional tax revenue to state and local governments, including help for a "school revenue problem,"[110] it unsurprisingly had little to no effect on the bootlegging and sale of hard liquor and seemed to have had no impact on the ongoing crime wave.[111]

In February 1933, Congress passed a resolution advocating for the repeal of Prohibition and nullification of the Volstead Act. The resolution required

As the Great Depression wore on, the legalization of beer became as much an economic as a moral argument. *From the* Greensboro Record, *November 23, 1932.*

statewide referendums for the appointment of a slate of electors to vote on approval of what would become the Twenty-First Amendment to the Constitution at special state conventions. The North Carolina General Assembly passed a referendum for a November 7 vote as to whether North Carolina would even hold a convention.[112] The debate was long and heated. The dry side of the conflict continued putting forth Prohibition as a moral imperative, while the traditionally wets made the economic recovery argument to the public.

The leaders of the repeal movement were centered in the Triad, with their initial meetings held at the King Cotton Hotel in Greensboro and later ones scheduled for High Point.[113] All the wrangling and newspaper predictions of a tight election came to naught, as after the November 7 referendum the eligible voters of North Carolina chose by a more than 2–1 margin of 293,484 to 120,190 to become the only state to reject holding a convention.[114] In the Triad, every county voted to not hold the convention. One month later, Utah became the thirty-sixth state to ratify the Twenty-First Amendment, and federal Prohibition finally came to an end.

POST-PROHIBITION AND THE ALCOHOL BEVERAGE CONTROL LAW

The repeal of the Eighteenth Amendment and the Volstead Act did not bring an end to alcohol prohibition in North Carolina, as all local option and state laws remained in effect, including statewide prohibition itself in the form of the Turlington Act. Only beer and wine of less than 3.2% alcohol could be purchased within the state. It took until 1935 for North Carolina to start dismantling prohibition bit by bit, with the result being a series of laws that affected the alcohol industry into the twenty-first century. In early 1935, the General Assembly passed a short single-paragraph law change that increased the maximum alcohol by volume in beer from 3.2 to 5.0%.[115] This change alone led to the planning of the never-opened Premier Brewing Company in High Point, Old South Brewing Company in Statesville and the Atlanta-owned Atlantic Brewing Company in Charlotte, south of the Triad.

The most consequential piece of post-Prohibition legislation to pass the General Assembly was the Alcohol Beverage Control Law in 1937, which still governs alcohol sales and distribution in North Carolina to this day.[116] The law elevated the maximum ABV for beer in the state to 6.0%, a cap that remained in place until 2005. The primary focus of the law, however, was to set up the State Board of Alcohol Control (ABC Board), with a broad range of responsibilities and powers to provide for the sale of liquor over 21.0% alcohol by volume through ABC-controlled liquor stores. Local option elections would determine whether a state-administered and county-managed store would be allowed in a community, with the alternative being that the county would remain governed by the Turlington Act. This legislation also set up North Carolina's three-tier system for alcohol in the state, enforcing a separation between the production, distribution and retailing aspects of the industry and initiating a state monopoly over the sale of hard liquor.

With the enactment of the ABC law, North Carolina finally began moving past its long alcohol prohibition, with legislation in place that would govern the beer industry for the next fifty years or more. In 1937, brewery payrolls were $105,340,229. By the end of the 1930s, the industry was bringing $9,380,000 in business to the state annually.[117] Though it would be a long, slow climb for the industry to get to where it is today, the groundwork was laid for a successful future.

4

BIG BEER COMES TO THE TRIAD

The end of Prohibition did not mean that on December 5, 1933, everything was suddenly exactly as it had been before, particularly in North Carolina. North and South Carolina ultimately voted against repeal, and the full statewide apparatus for allowing alcohol sales was not in place until 1937. Local option provisions pushed sales and distribution back even further and kept alcohol entirely off the table in many counties.

BUYING BEER AFTER PROHIBITION

As the 1930s advanced, however, it became easier to find beer in the state. Distributors like R.H. Barringer sprang into action to supply bars, cafés, roadhouses and retail stores as early as 1933. Pender's, a regional grocery chain, was advertising "ale or beer" (no brand specified) at nine cents per bottle in 1936, and Atlantic Pilsner was promoted that same year as "a 10¢ beer made the 15¢ way," suggesting competition based on price was already common.[118]

Beer and wine could also be had at some soda fountains, such as Rood's in downtown Greensboro, which offered properly cooled beer, wine and "any drink that's legal!"[119] During this time, most bars avoided referring to themselves as a "bar" or "saloon." Instead, "café" or "grill" were often the terms used by outlets providing on-site consumption of alcohol. Greensboro and Winston-Salem had dozens of cafés, lunchrooms and grills in 1938, and it is a safe bet that many if not most served beer. Neither city had an institution that called itself a "bar" or "saloon" (although Greensboro did have Little Tavern, a sandwich shop). Roadhouses, such as the Audree-Lee on the Greensboro-Burlington Road, provided similar service outside the cities.[120]

Even though liquor sales were an option as early as 1937, Greensboro and Winston-Salem did not get municipally owned (and state licensed) "ABC stores" until the early 1950s. Referenda in both cities in 1951 resulted in their first legal liquor sales in over forty years, with each city's stores agreeing to split a certain amount of revenue with the county. "For" votes outnumbered "against" in Greensboro by a margin of 11,176 to 6,724 on June 5, 1951, and multiple stores in each city opened just a few months later. High Point, Jamestown and many other cities and towns in the region eventually added liquor stores as well, though there are still several "dry" areas in the Triad.[121]

The Triad's two dominant beer distributors date from the years surrounding the end of Prohibition. R.H. Barringer Distributing was established in 1933 in Greensboro and was selling newly legalized low-alcohol beer and ale by 1934. Barringer obtained the franchise for Anheuser-Busch products in 1935, and the massive brewer provided most of the distributor's inventory until 2007, when Barringer began diversifying through acquisitions and new relationships with craft brewers.[122]

H.G. Wright Distributing was established in 1939 and purchased by I.H. Caffey in 1962. In the early days, only Miller, Falstaff and Country Club Malt Liquor were sold, and the company had only four employees. Beginning in the late 1980s, I.H. Caffey began acquisitions of other distributors and building relationships with new breweries, resulting in it becoming the largest distributor of Miller products in the Carolinas and Virginia. Caffey also partnered with craft brewers in the area, including Foothills Brewing Company in Winston-Salem.[123]

BEER PRODUCTION AFTER PROHIBITION

Corporate manufacturing of beer was slow to arrive in the area. Bottling and distribution operations dated as far back as the turn of the century with the Robert Portner Brewing Company, but the Triad did not have a pre-Prohibition history of large local brewing operations like cities of the Northeast and the Midwest.

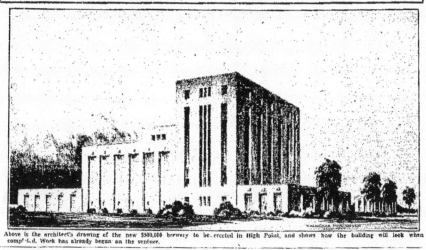

New $500,000 Brewery In High Point To Serve South

Above is the architect's drawing of the new $500,000 brewery to be erected in High Point, and shows how the building will look when completed. Work has already begun on the venture.

A rendering by brewery architect Waldemar Mortensen of the proposed Premier Brewing facility (never constructed) in High Point. *From* Burlington Daily Times-News, *January 19, 1935.*

One of the earliest planned brewery operations in the Triad came from the Premier Brewing Company. The Premier Brewing Company was incorporated in High Point in 1935 with capital stock of $412,500.[124] J. Berke von Linde was Premier's master brewer and learned his craft in Germany and the United States. The brewery, to have been designed by noted brewery architect Waldemar Mortensen, was planned to start with fifty thousand barrels annual production, with potential for expansion. Plans ultimately fell through, and the brewery never opened.[125]

While Premier Brewing Company's High Point facility never materialized, other major beer producers moved into the area beginning in the 1960s. Largely, this growth stemmed from the Triad's position as a regional transportation hub, a role that dated back to the 1800s when train lines converged alongside the Cascade Saloon on Elm Street in downtown Greensboro and the Portner Brewing Company placed "beer depots" right by the tracks there and in Winston. By the mid-1960s, railway transport was being supplanted by the interstate highway system, and the Triad was perfectly positioned to benefit from this, with the north–south Interstate 85 intersecting Greensboro and High Point, and the east–west Interstate 40 crossing both Greensboro and Winston-Salem.

When coupled with North Carolina's location as the north–south midpoint along the East Coast, it is not surprising that the major national brewers started looking to the Triad as a perfect location with distribution and expansion potential. It took some starts and stops, however, before corporate beer manufacturing would take hold in the Triad.

ANHEUSER-BUSCH COMPANY

In the spring of 1967, Anheuser-Busch announced alongside members of the Greensboro and High Point Chambers of Commerce that it was planning a brewery near the small Triad community of Jamestown, situated between the two larger Triad cities. The proposal included a $40 million brewery on a 400-acre lot, priced at $3,000 per acre, for a $1.2 million land purchase.[126] The brewery would be situated west of Greensboro and northwest of Interstate 85 between the Vickery Chapel Road and Groometown Road interchanges, employ 320 and produce 1.5 million barrels of beer annually. The brewery itself was estimated to encompass up to 80 acres of the 400-acre lot, with two years needed for construction.[127]

By fall of the same year, the project was in question. An engineer's report was released labeling the site as "undesirable for industrial development from the standpoint of water and sewer services." Greensboro officials claimed that the report was misinterpreted, and went on to note that Winston-Salem, because of its then-competing Schlitz Brewery project, would "just love to make something out of this."[128] Greensboro Chamber of Commerce Industrial Department manager John Parramore added that Anheuser-Busch was aware of the report, and due to its heavy and ongoing investments in the area, would be going ahead with construction.[129]

Nevertheless, by December 1967, Anheuser-Busch announced that it was postponing construction of the brewery indefinitely. The spokespeople attributed the postponement to a change in their East Coast distribution plans, and the belief that their under-construction Jacksonville, Florida brewery could handle their needed capacity.[130] Greensboro officials attributed this to cost overruns experienced by Anheuser-Busch in constructing two previous breweries, including the Jacksonville location, as well as increased financing costs. Officials went on to state that the earlier engineering report had nothing to do with the change in plans by the brewer. Whatever the reason, the indefinite postponement was just that, and the project never broke ground.[131] Today, the Grandover Resort and Conference Center resides in the proposed location.

JOSEPH SCHLITZ BREWING COMPANY

Around the same time that Anheuser-Busch was exploring plans to open a brewery in the Jamestown area, Schlitz turned its eye toward Winston-Salem. At the time, Schlitz was the second-largest brewer in the country, and it was looking to expand its production capacity. North Carolina's position on the East Coast, coupled with the cheaper real estate costs and labor, made it an ideal location. The first property that the company investigated was in Durham, but after the city refused to sell the water to the brewery,[132] Schlitz explored both Greensboro and Charlotte before settling on Winston-Salem.[133]

The company selected a lot of real estate at 145 Barnes Road, just off N.C. 52 and south of Interstate 40. This area was also easily served by the Winston-Salem Southbound Railway. The project was formally announced on June 29, 1967, with construction scheduled to begin in August. It had an estimated date of completion in 1969 with construction costs on the expansive 150 acres estimated at $40 million.[134] Annual production was planned at 2 million barrels per year.[135]

In the end, the brewery took thirty months to complete, and construction cost was closer to $60 million.[136] The brewery's capacity ended up over double the initial 2.0-million-barrel estimate at an astounding 4.4 million barrels per year of potential production.[137] The brewery itself was over 1.2 million square feet, not only the largest production facility built by Schlitz but also the largest brewery in the world at that time.[138] Additionally, the project was the largest single industrial

Souvenir stein commemorating the May 8, 1970 dedication of the Schlitz brewery in Winston-Salem. *Well Crafted NC.*

investment in Forsyth County's history[139] and the largest manufacturing plant of any kind in the whole of North Carolina.[140]

The brewery opened for operation on May 8, 1969, with a press tour, open house and two evenings of free entertainment for the community[141] and included a 135-foot-long hospitality space, taproom and kitchen called "The Brown Bottle," modeled after the architecture of Old Salem.[142] A month later, the facility already employed 190 workers, who at the time selected the Teamsters Union over the United Brewery Workers as their labor representatives.[143] Soon the employee count would rise to 450.[144]

By 1973, Schlitz controlled over 15% of the beer market in the United States. It was brewing more efficiently and cheaply in Winston-Salem than elsewhere. As a result, the company closed its Brooklyn brewery that March and announced the addition of more canning facilities at the Winston-Salem plant.[145]

At the same time the company was experiencing these highs, there were clouds on the horizon that would eventually lead to the dissolution of Schlitz Brewing. As early as 1972, a federal grand jury and the Securities and Exchange Commission were both investigating Schlitz marketing practices, leading to

Postcard showcasing the Brown Bottle guest facility at the Winston-Salem Schlitz plant. Note the Old Salem-influenced décor. *Well Crafted NC.*

747 indictments in 1978 for illegally marketing products and restraint of trade.[146] Infamously, in 1973, the company changed the recipe for its beer as a cost-cutting measure. It began using corn syrup to replace a percentage of barley and hop pellets as a substitute for fresh hops.[147] Schlitz also started decreasing the amount of time it allowed its beer to age, resulting in a protein haze developing in the normally clean beer as it chilled.[148] The beleaguered company began looking into adding anti-haze adjuncts to combat the hazing, instead of simply increasing the aging period of the beer. Schlitz ultimately selected a product called "Chill-Garde" that caused more problems than it solved. As it turned out, Chill-Garde had a chemical reaction with another Schlitz adjunct, a foam stabilizer called Kelcoloid used in bottles and cans after packaging. This reaction produced an accumulation of white flecks of released proteins in the beer. As the beer sat on shelves, the white flecks would clump together into a mucinous gelatin.[149] Ultimately, Schlitz was forced to recall and dispose of $1.4 million of packaged beer in 1976.[150]

When combined with the 1978 federal indictments, neither the company nor its reputation ever recovered. That same year, Miller Brewing surpassed Schlitz in sales to become the second-largest brewer in the country. By 1980, Schlitz had slipped further, with Pabst Brewing Company passing it in sales.[151]

Former Schlitz/Stroh's brewery on Barnes Road in Winston-Salem as it appears in 2021. *Well Crafted NC.*

On June 10, 1982, the end came when Stroh Brewery Company purchased Schlitz for $500 million.[152] Stroh's continued operating the Winston-Salem brewery, producing 5.5 million cases of beer a month,[153] but went into debt due to the Schlitz acquisition.

In February 1999, Stroh's announced the sale of most of its labels to Pabst, including Stroh's, Old Milwaukee, Schlitz and others.[154] The company was completely dissolved by 2000. The Winston-Salem brewery shut down operations on August 6, 1999.[155] The following year, the site was purchased and renovated into a business park.[156] At the time of its August shutdown, the brewery still produced over 5 million cases of beer a month, and Bill Abt, the former plant manager, estimated that in its thirty years of operation, the facility produced around 2 billion cases of beer and contributed $4.5 billion to the Triad economy.[157]

MILLER BREWING COMPANY

In 1975, when Schlitz was tackling its self-inflicted troubles, Miller Brewing Company began looking to North Carolina for brewery expansion. Much like Schlitz, it first looked to the Triangle area but was rebuffed by the Raleigh Chamber of Commerce, which was opposed to Miller's unionized workforce.[158] By September of that year, Miller had begun negotiations with representatives of the city of Eden in Rockingham County. On June 29, 1976, it publicly announced intentions to build a new production facility in the Triad city.[159] This project would become one of the largest capital investments the state had ever seen.[160]

Miller purchased 1,600 acres of farmland and began work on a facility capable of producing 3.0 million barrels of beer a year.[161] The project had estimated completion date in 1980 and a total project cost of $132 million.[162] Locally, the Christian Action League pushed against the development, but protests were quickly rebuffed by Rockingham County and Eden city officials.[163] By the time Miller opened for employment applications in March 1977, over five thousand people had applied for jobs at the new facility.[164] Four months later, on July 7, Miller president John Murphy announced an expansion to the still-in-progress project, increasing estimated production capacity from 3.0 to 8.8 million barrels per year. This capacity growth increased Miller's total investment in the facility by $250 million, with total estimated economic impact in the area near $112 million.[165]

Construction underway at the Miller Brewing facility in Eden. *Rockingham Community College Foundation, Inc., Historical Collections, Gerald B. James Library.*

Though the facility was not yet fully complete (full brewing operations were set to begin by the end of 1979), initial production began in March 1978.[166] At the time, the plant employed 1,400 Teamsters Union 321[167] workers, just shy of the projected 1,500 capacity. They produced approximately 750 million cans of beer a year.[168] On October 12, 1979, Miller announced yet another $21 million expansion to the location, increasing capacity to 10 million barrels per year and adding up to 200 more jobs. The company also established a new can manufacturing plant in neighboring Reidsville, bringing its investment in the state to over $300 million.[169]

One of the five thousand people hoping for employment in 1977 was thirty-year-old Patricia "Pat" Henry.[170] A Reidsville native and graduate of Bennett College, a historically Black college for women in Greensboro,[171] Henry left a position with DuPont in Martinsville, Virginia, to return to North Carolina. Though she had no experience in the brewing industry, she did hold a degree in chemical engineering from Bennett, and the Miller interviewer thought her résumé showed potential as a brewmaster. In 1977,

Henry was hired by Miller as a brewing supervisor.[172] She noted that on November 21, 1977, her first day of work at the Miller plant, "there were no workers. They didn't even have the walls up in the brew house." While Henry would eventually manage a team of four production brewers, she and the other supervisors initially worked the line themselves until Miller was able to hire employees to handle the job.[173]

In 1983, Henry was promoted to head of the bottling operation. In 1992, after completing a three-month course at the Siebel Institute of Technology, she fulfilled her interviewer's prediction and became brewmaster at Miller. This promotion made her the first female brewmaster at a major brewery in the country.[174] In this role, Henry supervised the work of forty production brewers. In 1994, she was again promoted, this time to packaging manager, supervising 330 employees and fourteen production lines.[175]

The following year, she was promoted once again, taking on the role of plant manager and overseeing the entire Miller operation in Eden. Once again, Henry was a trailblazer, becoming the first woman to hold this role at a U.S. brewery.[176] Reflecting on this, Henry said:

> To be a couple of firsts in this business that in the past has predominantly been male dominated, that's something that I'm very proud of. I look at it as, whether as a trailblazer or not, I want to make sure that what I'm doing will make it easier if my daughter wanted to come into something like this or anybody coming in behind me.[177]

Under Henry's leadership, the Eden brewery was the third most profitable of Miller's brewing operations. When employee morale dropped due to changes in the industry, Miller's faltering profits and threats of layoffs, Henry changed policies to allow employees to fish in the company pond and hunt in the surrounding woods.[178] She was also respected by the union leaders at the brewery, with locals president Jack Cipriani noting that he had "known her over twenty years. The one thing that has impressed me about her is her character. She keeps her word." Another union representative said that "her actions have demonstrated that you can trust her."[179] Henry left the Eden brewery in 2005 to become Miller's director of strategic projects.

By the early 2000s, Miller's standing in the U.S. beer market was slipping, and this decline was reflected in the Eden operation. In 2000, the company was producing 450,000 cases of beer a day.[180] Two years later, that number decreased to only 4,000.[181] By 2002, Miller's market share had been on the decline for three consecutive years, and with only 695 employees, it

Aerial view of the Miller Brewery in Eden. *Rockingham Community College Foundation, Inc., Historical Collections, Gerald B. James Library.*

Former Miller Brewing plant in Eden as it appeared in 2021. *Well Crafted NC.*

was operating at less than half of the workforce required back in the late 1970s.[182] By 2011, that number was down to 600, and the brewery focused primarily on brewing and distributing products from Miller's new craft beer portfolio, which included Blue Moon.[183] In September 2015, Anheuser-Busch completed a $100 billion acquisition of SABMiller and divested the Miller brands out to Molson Coors.[184] Just days later, the newly renamed MillerCoors announced that the Eden plant would cease operations in September 2016 after thirty-seven years of operation.[185]

At the time of its closure in 2016, MillerCoors was the third-largest employer in Rockingham County, and 520 people lost their jobs as a result.[186] The facility remains unused as of January 2021, but there is a glimmer of hope on the horizon. In late 2020, Nestle Purina PetCare Co. announced its intention to acquire and renovate the space into a dog food production facility by 2022, bringing 300 much-needed jobs and a $450 million investment to the community.[187]

THE COMING CHANGE

After Prohibition, the homebrewing of beer was illegal at the federal level. In 1976, while both Schlitz and Miller Brewing were running or opening major breweries in the Triad, a small group of homebrewers in California were lobbying Senator Alan Cranston for change.[188] Two years later and in coordination with Representative William Steiger of Wisconsin, they introduced Amendment No. 5354 into a transportation bill, H.R. 1337.[189] The amendment legalized the homebrewing of beer and exempted home-brewed beer from the excise taxes normally levied on alcohol, while creating a maximum output annually of up to two hundred gallons per household.

On October 14, 1978, President Jimmy Carter signed H.R. 1337 into law, and it went into effect on February 1, 1979 as Public Law 95-458. As people learned and grew their craft, the number of breweries in the United States began to expand quickly, and within fifteen years there was an 853% increase in their number across the country.[190] The first brewpub boom was underway.

Although Public Law 95-458 began changing the brewing landscape at the national level, state and local option laws across the country remained in place. This included North Carolina—at least until a German immigrant named Uli Bennewitz was convinced by his brother in 1985 that he should open a brewpub on the North Carolina coast.

5

THE BREWPUB BOOM

While the larger national and international beer companies continued building and brewing in North Carolina, the "microbrew" movement that had taken hold on the West Coast of the United States was rolling into North Carolina. In 1980, German immigrant Uli Bennewitz moved to Eastern North Carolina, initially working as a farm manager and agricultural land developer in the small community of Engelhard on the Pamlico Sound. He received a call from his brother in Munich, Germany, offering to sell him some brewery equipment. Bennewitz, missing the beer of his home country, bought the equipment and had it shipped to North Carolina, hoping to open a small restaurant and brewery in Manteo, the city in which he had his wife had settled. It was only after making the equipment purchase that Bennewitz realized that there was a hitch in his plan. The State of North Carolina did not allow breweries to sell their beer to customers on-site.[191]

Undeterred, Bennewitz worked with the state's Alcoholic Beverage Control Commission to change the law of North Carolina and open the doorway for the craft beer industry. Bennewitz, who was in the United States on an expired visitor's visa at the time, crafted language to expand the existing laws permitting on-site winery sales to allow for on-site brewery sales. State senator Marc Basnight of Manteo sponsored Senate Bill 536 in 1985, framing it as a bill supporting what Bennewitz called "a little hobby project on the Outer Banks."[192] The bill, titled "An Act to Allow On-Premise

Above: The bottling of Buckshot Amber at the Natty Greene's Brewing Co. production facility. *Natty Greene's Brewing Co.*

Left: Uli Bennewitz, owner of the Weeping Radish Brewing Co., changed North Carolina law to allow for the on-premises sale of beer. *Well Crafted NC.*

Sales of Beer at Mini-Breweries," was passed in the North Carolina House in June and the Senate in July.[193]

On July 4, 1985, the State of North Carolina officially opened its doors for the micro-beer revolution. Bennewitz led the way when he opened Weeping Radish Brewing in Manteo the following year. He opened a second Weeping Radish location in Durham in 1988. Greenshields Brewery in Raleigh and Dilworth Brewing in Charlotte followed, both opening in 1989.

LOGGERHEAD BREWING COMPANY

The Triad region became home to North Carolina's fifth craft brewpub in April 1990 when Loggerhead Brewing Company opened its doors in Greensboro. Housed in a strip mall on Vandalia Road near the intersection of Interstates 40 and 85 in southwest Greensboro, Loggerhead was described in *All About Beer* magazine as having "little going for it in terms of street appeal. But once inside, you'll forget about the entrance way."[194]

Led by Gary Vickers, a chemist who had worked as a brewing supervisor at the Miller Brewing Company facility in Eden, Loggerhead was a restaurant and bar that focused on brewing by traditional Bavarian purity laws, restricting ingredients to malted barley, hops, yeast and water. Vickers and assistant brewmaster Duane Abbott focused on producing four main house beers. As described in the Loggerhead menu, the brewery featured the Loggerhead Pilsner, a "light-bodied American style beer"; the General Greene Lager, "a deep amber lager with a rich and malty body"; the Loggerhead Light, a "full flavored pilsner with ⅓ the calories"; and the most popular, the Gate City Ale, "a full-bodied brew with a taste all its own."[195]

In addition to its four standard beers, Loggerhead included "specialty brews," more limited seasonal brews and variations such as a sweeter cherry-flavored beer available during the first months of operation. A "sampler tray" flight of the four standard beers and one specialty brew was available for $2.50.[196]

Largely because brewing and serving beer on site was a novelty in North Carolina, the Loggerhead restaurant and menu designs stressed that the beer was produced in house and educated consumers on how the beer was made. The restaurant space featured ceiling-high glass windows that allowed customers to look into the brewing space.[197] The menu included a full-page description of the brewing process, including hand-drawn illustrations labeling the various stainless-steel tanks and equipment the customers could see.[198]

After some initial struggles with funding, Loggerhead's brewing operations continued, but the restaurant side of the business did not. In 1994, Loggerhead shifted its focus solely to beer production, signing a contract to supply beer at two local Ham's Restaurants in January and closing the restaurant operations completely in April. As Vickers noted in an interview with the *Greensboro News & Record*, the restaurant side of the business had been struggling, and they made the decision to "go with our strong suit" by focusing solely on brewing operations.[199]

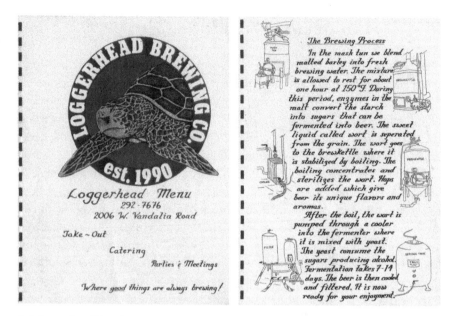

Left: Loggerhead Brewing Co. in Greensboro was the fifth brewpub to open in the state. This is a menu from its Vandalia Road location. *Well Crafted NC.*

Right: A hand-written and illustrated explanation of the "The Brewing Process" at Loggerhead Brewing Co. in Greensboro, from the interior of their brewpub menu. *Well Crafted NC.*

By early 1995, Loggerhead had dissolved, but its legacy continued with Gate City Brewing. With Vickers still serving as brewmaster, Gate City Brewing was a subsidiary of Ham's Restaurants and focused solely on making beer for numerous Ham's Restaurants across the region. The number of beers made was reduced from five to two: Charley's Barley, a light lager, and Gate City Ale, a pale ale.[200]

Spring Garden Brewing Company

In 1991, Greensboro saw the development of its second microbrewery when restaurateur Bill Sherrill chose to open Spring Garden Brewing Company. Located near Guilford College, Spring Garden Brewing grew out of Sherrill's Spring Garden Bar and Grill restaurants, casual dining restaurants with locations in Greensboro, Winston-Salem, Charlotte and Chapel Hill. After visiting more than eighty brewpubs across the country and participating

The original Spring Garden Brewing Co. location near Guilford College in Greensboro, before it moved to Whitsett and changed its name to Red Oak Brewery. *Red Oak Brewery.*

in the Institute for Brewing Studies' tour of California breweries in 1989, Sherrill purchased a ten-barrel brewing system and hired Canadian brewer Christian Boos to lead the brewing operations for Spring Garden.[201]

Spring Garden's space was eclectic, described in the *New Brewer* magazine as providing customers "with the genteel hospitality of a summer home tucked somewhere in the Blue Ridge Mountains."[202] Decorative elements included an antique Indian motorcycle, large paintings by artists Alan Wolton and Jack Ketner and a mural over the brew kettle that was painted to resemble the ceiling of the Sistine Chapel, with God handing Man a pint of beer.

As with Loggerhead, Spring Garden featured traditional German beers brewed according to Bavarian purity standards. At opening, the menu featured two house-brewed beers: Hummin' Bird Extra Light Lager and Oak Ridge Amber. Both beers sat at approximately 3% ABV. Beers from other national breweries, such as Rolling Rock and Miller Lite, were also sold. Soon, however, Sherrill recognized that Spring Garden's own beers were selling well enough to begin removing the other beers from the menu. Boos

Left: Red Oak Brewery brochure cover. *Red Oak Brewery.*

Above: An original Spring Garden Brewing Co. Hummin' Bird Lager coaster. Note the espousal of the 1516 Bavarian Purity Law. *Red Oak Brewery.*

stated, "We started out selling a lot of Miller, and then when we came out with Hummin' Bird, Miller sales went down. When we lightened Hummin' Bird, Miller sales went down even further."[203]

The interest in Spring Garden's house-brewed beers continued to grow, and more beers were added to the portfolio. Those included Battlefield Bock, a dark lager, and Hummingbird, a pilsner (now a helles lager). The most popular beer at Spring Garden, however, was its Red Oak, a Vienna-style amber lager created by Boos. The Red Oak became so popular that, in 2001, Sherrill changed the brewery's name from Spring Garden to Red Oak, recognizing their most popular brew.[204]

In 2000, Sherrill began plans to expand the brewery's production capacities with a new facility in Whitsett in eastern Guilford County. Through its multiple distribution accounts, Spring Garden Brewing had outgrown its initial brewing space, where it produced between 3,500 and 4,000 gallons per week. Sherrill's company paid $675,000 for new land in the Rock Creek Corporate Center along Interstate 85/40, outside of the Greensboro city limits. The new development, however, would not come immediately. In 2002, Boos left Red Oak and the brewing industry. Sherrill

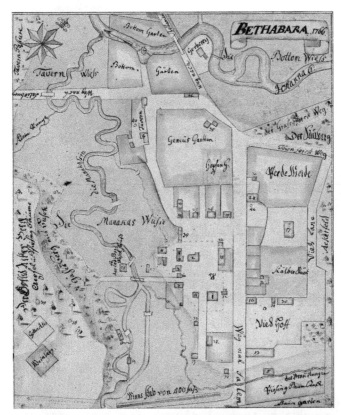

Left: Map of Bethabara Town Lot by Christian Gottlieb Reuter, 1766. The brewery is along the stream to the bottom right. *Moravian Archives, Winston-Salem, North Carolina.*

Below: The Herrman Buttner House at Bethabara, Winston-Salem, the rebuilt home of the Bethabara brewer and distiller. Completed on September 14, 1803. *Well Crafted NC.*

Former Schlitz/Stroh's brewery on Barnes Road in Winston-Salem as it appeared in 2021. *Well Crafted NC.*

Former Miller Brewing plant in Eden as it appeared in 2021. *Well Crafted NC.*

Right: Loggerhead Brewing Co. twenty-two-ounce Gate City Ale bottle. Located in Greensboro, Loggerhead was the fifth brewpub to open in the state. *Well Crafted NC.*

Below: Red Oak Brewery brochure. *Red Oak Brewery.*

Foothills Brewpub on Fourth Street in downtown Winston-Salem. *Erik Lars Myers.*

Interior, Natty Greene's Brewing Co. downtown Greensboro brewpub. *Erik Lars Myers.*

Top: Natty Greene's Brewing Co. twelve-ounce Mt. Mitchell single hop IPA bottle. *Well Crafted NC.*

Bottom: Red Oak Brewery Hummin' Bird Helles Lager bottle. *Well Crafted NC.*

Pop the Cap promotional brochure, advocating for the removal of the then-6% ABV cap on beer sold in North Carolina. *Sean Lily Wilson.*

NCCBG brochure promoting North Carolina as the "State of Southern Beer." *North Carolina Craft Brewers Guild.*

Left: The Red
Oak Lager Haus
in Whitsett. *Well
Crafted NC.*

Below: Brewmaster
Chris Buckley
among the tanks at
Red Oak Brewery
in Whitsett. *Red
Oak Brewery.*

The bottling line in action at Red Oak in Whitsett. *Red Oak Brewery.*

Foothills Brewery and Tasting Room at Kimwell Drive in Winston-Salem. *Erik Lars Myers.*

Angry Troll Brewing Co. in Elkin. *Well Crafted NC.*

The Hoots Beer Co. taproom in Winston-Salem. *Erik Lars Myers.*

Left: The original 1988 Pig Pounder beer from Darryl's, namesake of Pig Pounder Brewery in Greensboro. *Well Crafted NC.*

Below: The Gibb's Hundred Brewing Co. Lewis Street location in Greensboro before its move out of downtown. *Erik Lars Myers.*

Right: Schmidly Bock, named in honor of Steve Schmidly, who fought for a local ordinance allowing alcohol sales in Asheboro. *Four Saints Brewing Co.*

Below: Hand-painted, themed murals decorate the walls of the taproom at Fiddlin' Fish Brewing Co. in Winston-Salem. *Well Crafted NC.*

Left: The brewhouse at Haw River Farmhouse Ales in Saxapahaw. *Erik Lars Myers.*

Below: Wise Man Brewing Co. in Winston-Salem, housed in a 1929 warehouse and former Angelo Bros. Wholesale location. *Well Crafted NC.*

Pig Pounder Brewery in Greensboro. *Well Crafted NC.*

Joymongers Brewing Co. taproom in Greensboro. *Well Crafted NC.*

Top: A recently redesigned Sexual Chocolate Imperial Stout label from Foothills Brewing Co. *Well Crafted NC.*

Left: A full taproom at Little Brother Brewing Co. in downtown Greensboro. *Well Crafted NC.*

The site of a family-owned former bottling factory undergoing final renovations before opening as Greensboro's Oden Brewing Company in November 2019. *Well Crafted NC.*

Brown Truck Brewery, located on Main Street in High Point, is a winner of multiple GABF medals, including the 2016 "Very Small Brewer of the Year" award. *Well Crafted NC.*

During the COVID-19 pandemic, social distancing and masking were apparent at the Red Oak Lager Haus in Whitsett. *Red Oak Brewery.*

Grand opening celebration at the Goose and the Monkey Brewhouse in Lexington. It became the city's first brewery in 2020. *Well Crafted NC.*

The bottling line in action at Red Oak Brewery in Whitsett. *Red Oak Brewery.*

hired Henryk Orlik from Abita Brewing Company for a brief stint. Then, in March 2004, Chris Buckley was hired. Buckley would oversee the brewing operations at Red Oak as well as the design of the new brewing facility at the Rock Creek Corporate Center in Whitsett. In April 2007, the new facility opened, producing its first batch of Red Oak lager by July and distributing bottles of Red Oak and Hummingbird soon after.[205]

LIBERTY BREWERY AND GRILL

The craft brewpub scene in the Triad expanded beyond Greensboro in 2000 when Liberty Brewery and Grill opened in High Point. After paying $1.5 million for the new brewpub's site next to Oak Hollow Mall, an additional $30,000 was invested to transform the former site of a Red Robin restaurant into a space for brewing. Like Loggerhead and Spring Garden, Liberty's space was designed to showcase its brewing operations, with the copper brewhouse attached to the side of the brewpub and viewable behind a glass wall.

Liberty Steakhouse & Brewery in High Point. *Erik Lars Myers.*

Interior, Liberty Steakhouse & Brewery in High Point. *Erik Lars Myers.*

Unlike the two local-owned brewpubs in Greensboro, Liberty was a part of the T-Bonz Restaurant Group, based in South Carolina. Liberty opened its first location in Myrtle Beach in the mid-1990s. The High Point location was its second. At opening, Eric Lamb was hired from Mendocino Brewing Company in California to lead the brewing operations at the restaurant group's sole North Carolina location. Liberty's menu featured a mix of lagers and ales, with eight of its own beers on tap at opening, including a Red Rocket Ale and the Miss Liberty Lager.[206] Lamb left the High Point location to move to Liberty's Myrtle Beach brewpub in 2007, and Todd Isbell was hired to manage the brewing operations in High Point.[207]

Natty Greene's Brewing Company

In October 2003, UNC Greensboro alumni Kayne Fisher and Chris Lester announced plans to open Hamburger Square Brewhouse on South Elm Street in Greensboro. Fisher and Lester owned three other beer-centered restaurants in the area: Old Town Draft House and Tap Room Grill in Greensboro and First Street Draft House in Winston-Salem.[208] The thirteen-

The Natty Greene's Brewing Co. downtown Greensboro brewpub on South Elm Street, also former home of the R.P. Gorrell Saloon. *Erik Lars Myers.*

A selection of award-winning Natty Greene's beers. *Natty Greene's Brewing Co.*

thousand-square-foot building in downtown Greensboro, however, would allow them to move beyond selling craft beers to making their own. Scott Christoffel was brought in from Left Hand Brewing Company in Colorado to serve as the brewpub's first head brewer.

On August 1, 2004, the brewpub opened with a new name—Natty Greene's Pub and Brewing Company—an homage to Nathanael Greene, the Revolutionary War general for whom the city of Greensboro was named. Nearly 250 people waited outside of the brewpub when its doors opened.[209] Like Liberty, Natty Greene's focused on brewing ales and lagers, serving six different beers at opening. These included a pale ale, a stout and an amber. In 2006, its Old Town Brown earned a silver medal at the Great American Beer Festival in the English-style brown category.[210]

FOOTHILLS BREWING COMPANY

Both Greensboro and High Point had brewpubs by 2000, but it was not until 2004 that the plans for Winston-Salem's first brewpub were announced.

The interior of the Foothills brewpub on Fourth Street in downtown Winston-Salem. *Erik Lars Myers.*

Initially called 638 Brewing Company due to its planned location at 638 West Fourth Street in downtown Winston-Salem, the brewpub was developed by Bob Hiller, owner of Blue Ridge Brewing Company in Greenville, South Carolina; Jamie Bartholomaus, a brewer from Olde Hickory Brewing in Hickory, North Carolina; and two other local businessmen.[211]

Renovations at the historic building took longer than anticipated, but in March 2005, the newly renamed Foothills Brewing Company opened to the public. Bartholomaus served as the head brewer, offering seven different house-brewed ales at opening, including Pilot Mountain Pale Ale, Salem Gold and Torch Pilsner. Foothills also emphasized the restaurant side of the brewpub, serving sandwiches as well as higher-priced entrees featuring steak or various game meats.[212]

Soon after opening, Foothills' beers began winning awards at major craft beer festivals. The Baltic Porter took gold at the 2006 Great American Beer Festival. At the 2008 Brewers Association World Beer Cup in San Diego, People's Porter won a gold medal, while Total Eclipse Stout took silver.[213]

Bartholomaus quickly began distributing kegs of Foothills beer to various restaurants and bars in the region, initially saving only one beer for bottling.

Top: Foothills People's Porter bottle label. *Foothills Brewing Co.*

Bottom: The Foothills brewpub on Fourth Street in downtown Winston-Salem. *Erik Lars Myers.*

Foothills' Sexual Chocolate Imperial Stout was first released in bottles in February 2008 as a limited edition of only five hundred hand-numbered bottles. The previous year it had been available only in the taproom. As one of the earliest brewpub bottle release events in the Southeast, those five hundred bottles sold out in forty-nine minutes.[214]

Beer-Related Businesses

In addition to seeing the opening of the earliest brewpubs in the Triad, the 1990s and early 2000s gave rise to the growth of numerous local businesses that catered to the burgeoning craft beer community in the region. Businesses like the Ale and Beer Supply Company, operated out of School Kids Records on Spring Garden Street in Greensboro, saw a sharp increase in the number of people interested in learning how to brew their own beer at home.[215] Homebrew clubs like the Winston-Salem Wort Hawgs, founded in 1994, and the Greensboro-based Battleground Brewers Guild, founded in 2000, were created for members to learn more about the art of brewing and beer appreciation.[216]

The growing local interest in homebrewing was coupled with a growth in the distribution in the Triad of craft beers created outside of North Carolina. This included the opening of microbrew-centric draft houses like Old Town Draught House. Old Town, opened by Kayne Fisher and Chris Lester in Greensboro in 1996, featured seventeen different American microbrews on draft. Fisher and Lester continued by opening First Street Draft House in Winston-Salem in 1998.[217] Later, the duo opened Natty Greene's Brewing Company in downtown Greensboro.

Companies like Hog's Head Beer Cellars, which opened in 1995, also sprang up to provide mail-order "microbrew of the month" subscription services. Headed by Jim Lowe and Polly Nelson of Greensboro, Hog's Head Beer Cellars sent subscribers two different six packs of craft beer each month from breweries across the United States. Also included in the monthly shipment was a newsletter, providing information about the included breweries and other beer-related news.[218] Hog's Head closed in 2000, selling its membership list to World Beer Direct of Massachusetts.[219]

The first craft beer festival in the Triad region began in Greensboro in 2005. The first annual Summertime Brews Festival, sponsored by local radio station Rock 92 and organized by the station's program director Dave Aiken,

A jam-packed 2011 Foothills Sexual Chocolate Imperial Stout pre-release party. A line down the block would form at the brewpub the next morning. *Steve Kim.*

brought nearly two thousand people to the First Horizon Baseball Park, the stadium of the Greensboro Grasshoppers, to sample beers from across the country.[220] All of the local breweries in operation at the time—Red Oak, Liberty, Natty Greene's and Foothills—participated alongside national breweries like Brooklyn Brewing from New York and SweetWater Brewery from Georgia.[221]

Individual residents even helped develop the Triad region's reputation as a site where craft beer was recognized and appreciated. The 2001 "Beer Drinker of the Year" title, bestowed by Wynkoop Brewing Company in Colorado, went to a Triad resident. Cornelia Corey of Clemmons was the first woman to win the national award, which is based on a combination of beer knowledge and enthusiasm. Her husband, Roy, followed by claiming the title in 2003.[222]

Pop the Cap

While the craft beer industry was beginning to take hold in the Triad, beer enthusiasts and professionals across the state lobbied for the revision of a law that placed an upper limit of 6% alcohol by volume (ABV) on any beers made or sold in North Carolina. The law, which had been in place since the passage of the 1937 Alcoholic Beverage Control Act, severely limited the styles of beer that could be served across the state. In 2002, a coalition known as "Pop the Cap" raised money and hired a lobbyist to help push a bill through the state legislature that would remove—or at least increase—this limit on a beer's ABV.

The "Pop the Cap" movement was a statewide initiative, with Sean Lily Wilson (current owner of Fullsteam Brewery in Durham) serving as the nonprofit organization's president and Julie Johnson Bradford (then the co-owner and editor of Durham-based *All About Beer* magazine) serving as director. In the Triad region, Kipp Hollingsworth of Winston-Salem volunteered to lead the effort to rally support in the area for the ABV change. While many of the fundraising events for Pop the Cap were held in the Triangle, the Triad hosted its first benefit in May 2004 with a rockabilly concert at Ziggy's in Winston-Salem.[223]

An 11"x17" Pop the Cap poster celebrating the passage of HB 392, raising the ABV cap in North Carolina to 15%. *Kipp Hollingsworth.*

Initially, the movement focused on eliminating the ABV cap altogether. Two and a half years after the movement's start, a bill proposing the removal of the cap was introduced into the North Carolina legislature. During the legislative process, however, the proposed elimination of the cap was changed to a new, higher cap of 15%. This bill—House Bill 392—moved through the House and Senate and was officially signed into law by Governor Mike Easley on August 13, 2005.[224]

The advocates for the Pop the Cap bill estimated that changing North Carolina's ABV limit might create three hundred new jobs to the state. Within ten years of the bill's passage, however, North Carolina's total number of craft breweries exploded, with approximately three thousand new jobs created in breweries and thousands more in associated industries across the state.[225] Craft beer had taken hold across North Carolina, and the Triad region was set for a boom in this growing industry.

6

CRAFT BEER IN THE TRIAD TODAY

By 2013, North Carolina could boast the highest number of craft breweries in the South, with ninety craft breweries in operation across the state. The Triad region was home to three of the top five–producing craft breweries in the state—Natty Greene's in Greensboro (second), Foothills in Winston-Salem (third) and Red Oak in Whitsett (fifth). With Liberty in High Point added to the mix, it was estimated that the region's four craft breweries generated roughly $25 million annually in sales.[226]

LOCAL LAWS AND REGULATIONS

The passage of the Pop the Cap legislation in 2005 opened the doors in North Carolina to new beer styles. Coupled with a boom in homebrewing interest and a rising awareness of the value of shopping locally and supporting locally owned businesses, the interest in developing new craft breweries across the region expanded. Many cities and counties in the Triad, however, had local ordinances and laws that limited where new breweries could be located and how they could operate. Some areas restricted what types of industry might open in their main business districts. Some cities and counties remained dry, not allowing alcohol production or sale in their area. While these restrictions slowed the industry boom in the region, citizens across the Triad began to petition their local leaders for changes.

Construction underway at Little Brother Brewing, housed in the former home of the J.R. Stewart Saloon. Pictured here is Karmen Bulmer, general manager. *Little Brother Brewing Co.*

Co-owner Joel McClosky mans the taps at Four Saints Brewing Co. in Asheboro. *Erik Lars Myers.*

The city of Asheboro in Randolph County was the site of much political debate in 2008 as citizens went to the polls to vote on options that would allow alcohol sales in city limits. While Randolph County had been home to numerous moonshine stills over the years (the *Greensboro Daily News* reported that "at one point [between 1890–94], there were nineteen distilleries running full blast in Randolph County"),[227] bans on legal alcohol sales in the county traced back to the 1950s. From the 1960s through the 2000s, voters in Asheboro repeatedly voted against ballot initiatives that would legalize the sale of alcoholic beverages.

In 2008, citizens of Asheboro broke into two factions over the issue of alcohol sales—the Citizens for the Future of Asheboro, who supported alcohol sales, and the Citizens for a Safe and Healthy Asheboro, who opposed. The Citizens for the Future of Asheboro, led by many local business leaders, including the group's co-chairman and local lawyer Steve Schmidly, argued that the ban on alcohol sales limited economic growth in the town, preventing many restaurants, hotels and other businesses from opening in Asheboro. The Citizens for a Safe and Healthy Asheboro, on the other hand, were led by a number of local church leaders and argued that alcohol sales would do more harm than good in the community.

A series of referendums to allow different types of alcohol sales in Asheboro was placed on the ballot in July 2008. Tensions were high in the city on the day of the vote, with the Randolph County Board of Elections choosing to announce the results online due to fear of potential violence. On July 29, 2008, 54% of all registered voters in Asheboro (6,654 people) cast their ballots in this special election, which saw the initiatives in favor of alcohol sales succeed by more than 60% of the vote.[228] Local restaurants immediately began adding alcohol to their menu options, but it would not be until 2015 that a craft brewery (Four Saints Brewing Company, located on Fayetteville Street) opened its doors in Asheboro.

Local ordinances also restricted brewery operations and failed to recognize the changes in the industry as it moved from a brewpub model, where beer is brewed primarily to serve on-site at an affiliated restaurant, to a model that emphasized taproom sales and wholesale distribution. In Greensboro in 2013, local zoning ordinances allowed only a brewpub model to exist in the central business district. The ordinance definition of a "microbrewery" focused on small-scale production and off-site sales, and these types of businesses were relegated to the parts of the city zoned for industrial production. There was no consideration for on-site sales in a taproom.

Four Saints Brewing Co. opened in 2015 on Fayetteville Street in Asheboro, becoming Randolph County's first brewery. *Erik Lars Myers.*

Mark Gibb in the brewing facility at Gibb's Hundred Brewing's downtown Greensboro location. *Gibb's Hundred Brewing Co.*

Gibb's Hundred Brewing Co. original Lewis Street location in downtown Greensboro. *Gibb's Hundred Brewing Co.*

In January 2014, Mark Gibb proposed an amendment to the city's planning guidelines to change the definition of a microbrewery. Gibb was seeking to open a new brewery in Downtown Greensboro, but the zoning restrictions in place at the time would have required him to have a restaurant as part of his business in order to fit the city's definition of a "brewpub" and open in the downtown area. Gibb saw this as a restriction on his business plan, noting "the challenge there is that, well certainly for me and for many breweries today, is that they do want to have a substantial taproom and put it in a downtown location, where you can draw in a good crowd, but at the same time they want to sell a significant amount of beer wholesale."[229]

On February 18, 2014, the Greensboro City Council voted to make the changes proposed by Gibb. Specifically, the council added language to the local ordinance specifying that microbreweries would contain a taproom, defined by the city as "a room that is ancillary to the production of beer at a brewery, microbrewery, and brewpub where the public can purchase and/ or consume beer produced on site."[230] This change would open the doors for a craft beer boom in Downtown Greensboro, with five new craft breweries (including Gibb's own brewery on West Lewis Street, Gibb's Hundred Brewing Company) joining Natty Greene's in Greensboro over the next four years.

STUDYING BREWING SCIENCES AT RCC

While the doors opened for craft beer in the Triad region, many of the "big beer" facilities that operated in the area began to downsize and ultimately close. In 2011, Miller Brewing was Rockingham County's third-largest employer with hundreds of people on their payroll. After numerous reductions in staffing, the facility closed in 2016.

One lasting effect of these companies, however, can be seen in the growth of beer-related educational offerings at Rockingham Community College (RCC). The Industrial Technologies Department at RCC began offering homebrewing courses in 2011 as part of its continuing education series.[231] The demand for the class was high, both because of the specialized needs of the local Miller workforce as well as the growing interest in craft beer across the state. Two years later, RCC officially offered a Brewing, Distillation, and Fermentation program, becoming the first community college in the United States to offer a degree in the science and technology of brewing.[232]

The program relied on many local brewers and beer industry experts to teach the classes. This included Todd Isbell, head brewer at Liberty Brewery and Grill in High Point, who was among those approached by RCC to help design the program and teach courses. The program's curriculum was established in consultation with Isbell and other local brewers. Isbell recalled,

> *They came to me. I think they went to several different breweries in the area and were just looking for, it was really a reconnoiter, for lack of a better phrase, to just see what the interest was from the educational side. For example, if I was hiring an assistant, what would I want them to know? What would I want them to be trained in? A lot of people really wanted more of the hardware engineering infrastructure side of things. If this pump seal leaks, I want someone to be able to replace that without even worrying about it. Understand the basic refrigeration cycle. They have to understand brewing as well.*[233]

Another prominent instructor in the program was Cindy Vickers, a former microbiologist with MillerCoors whose husband, Gary, had opened the region's first brewpub, Loggerhead, in Greensboro in 1990. One of Vickers's teaching approaches was to bring in samples of Miller High Life and "spike them chemically so you could discover what acetaldehyde really is like, what diacetyl is, what isovaleric acid is, those kinds of things."[234] She

GABF Gold Winner!

Gibb's Hundred Brewing
One Year of Beer for Thought
Sat, Oct. 17th 1pm–8pm

Beer!
ELEVEN Gibb's Beers
-including-
New Release:
Squaring the Cirle
Barleywine
-and-
The Guilty Party ESB
GABF Gold Winner!

Food!
Spice Cantina
King Queen Haitian
Mellow Mushroom
Crafted: The Art of the Taco
Ghassan's
Empanadas Borinquen
Marty's BBQ
Irish Stew

Live Music!

The Ends   Colin Cutler   **THE RINALDI FLYING CIRCUS**

117 W Lewis St, Greensboro

Gibb's Hundred Brewing Co. one year anniversary poster. *Gibb's Hundred Brewing Co.*

would adjust the flaws introduced to the beer as a means of helping her students develop a palate for tasting and diagnosing these problems.

In August 2013, RCC officially opened its new Center for Brewing Sciences in Eden. Classes in the new program began in August 2013.[235]

Even after the closure of the Miller facility in September 2016, the RCC Brewing, Distillation and Fermentation program continued to grow. Both full associate of applied sciences degrees and certificates are offered, and many RCC graduates have moved on to ownership or operational positions at craft breweries across the region. For instance, Radar Brewing Company opened in Winston-Salem on New Year's Day 2020. Two of the co-owners, Aaron Wall and Aaron Sizemore, both took classes in the RCC program; Wall returned to teach as an adjunct instructor for two years.[236]

TRIAD BREWERS ALLIANCE

The North Carolina Craft Brewers Guild (NCCBG), a nonprofit organization focused on promoting North Carolina beer and breweries, was created in 2008 to serve as a statewide hub for brewers and brewery owners to build partnerships, exchange ideas, and advocate for legislative issues. Two Triad area brewing industry leaders were involved in the Guild's beginnings—Jamie Bartholomaus of Foothills Brewing Company in Winston-Salem and Sebastian Wolfrum of Natty Greene's Brewing Company in Greensboro.[237] The NCCBG developed marketing campaigns to brand North Carolina as "The State of Southern Beer," created festivals and brewing competitions to spotlight the work of North Carolina craft breweries, lobbied for April to be officially named "NC Beer Month," and sponsored an annual conference and continuing education opportunities for industry professionals.

As the craft brewing industry grew across North Carolina, brewers and brewery owners began to seek opportunities to engage in smaller, more localized professional organizations. In 2017, the Triad Brewers Alliance (TBA) was founded to provide a central hub for collaboration and promotion across breweries in an eleven-county radius. Joel McClosky of Four Saints Brewing Company in Asheboro served as the TBA's first president.

The TBA quickly grew, with members representing breweries that had been in operation since the mid-2000s to breweries that were in planning. For example, as Ashlee and Brent Moore worked to open the Goose and the Monkey Brewhouse in Lexington (that city's first craft brewery, which opened in 2020), they turned to the TBA to learn more about the brewing industry and meet local industry professionals who could help them work toward a successful opening.[238]

NCCBG and TBA promotional stickers. *North Carolina Craft Brewers Guild and Triad Brewers Alliance.*

Grand opening celebration at the Goose and the Monkey Brewhouse in Lexington. It became the city's first brewery in 2020. *Well Crafted NC.*

The TBA has also worked to promote the craft brewing industry in the region through special events and collaborations. To celebrate NC Beer Month in April 2017, nine TBA breweries (Liberty Brewery in High Point; Joymongers Brewing , Preyer Brewing, Gibb's Hundred Brewing and Natty Greene's Brewing in Greensboro; Wise Man Brewing in Winston-Salem; Four Saints Brewing in Asheboro; Angry Troll Brewing in Elkin; and Bull City Ciderworks in Lexington) collaborated to create the TBA Tripel as a way of celebrating the organization's founding and highlighting the industry across the area.[239]

In June 2017, the TBA sponsored its first festival in partnership with Downtown Greensboro, Inc. Dubbed "The Ultimate Triad Brewing Championship," the initial festival showcased six local breweries, all brewing beers centered on a special ingredient—cucumbers. Attendees received small samples of all the beers and cast votes for their favorite. Preyer Brewing Company won the title in 2017. In 2018, the festival name changed to the "Downtown Taste N Tap," and the breweries were teamed with local restaurants to create a small bite pairing. Lemons were the required ingredient for the seven competing breweries. Pig Pounder Brewing of Greensboro was named the 2018 winner.[240]

2014–2019: A Period of Growth

The craft beer community saw tremendous growth in the Triad between 2014 and 2019. In 2019, two new craft breweries joined the seven already in operation in Greensboro (SouthEnd Brewing Company and Oden Brewing Company). Six of those seven had just been opened in the previous four years (Pig Pounder and Gibb's Hundred in 2014, Preyer Brewing in 2015, Joymongers in 2016, Little Brother Brewing in 2017, and Leveneleven Brewing in 2018). Six new breweries joined Foothills in Winston-Salem (Hoots in 2013, Small Batch in 2014, Wise Man and Fiddlin' Fish in 2017, Incendiary in 2019 and Radar in 2020), with two more added to Liberty in High Point (Brown Truck in 2016 and Goofy Foot in 2018). Outside of the three major Triad cities, other towns in the region also welcomed new craft breweries during this time. Kernersville, Burlington, Elkin, Mount Airy, Saxapahaw, and more all saw new craft breweries pop up in their Triad towns.

In Asheboro, Randolph County, voters approved the sale of alcohol in their city limits in 2008. But it would take a few more years before a craft

Gibb's Hundred Brewing Co. Lewis Street brewhouse. *Erik Lars Myers.*

brewery opened. In 2008, Joel McClosky was a teacher in the Asheboro Public Schools, and one of his co-workers had a husband (Andrew Deming) who was a homebrewer. They began brewing together. In 2011, the two attended a downtown chili cookoff and noticed that there were no locally brewed beer options available. At that moment, they decided to bring a craft brewery to Asheboro. They chose the name Four Saints Brewing Company to honor four patron saints connected to beer and brewing (Saint Luke, Saint Augustine of Hippo, Saint Nicholas and Saint Wenceslaus).[241]

McClosky and Deming turned to Kickstarter to help raise funds for the brewery's opening, and in May 2015, they opened the doors of Four Saints in a building that had, decades before, served as home of the Hedrick Motor Company, a local car dealer and service center. That same year, two of their beers—the blonde and the hefeweizen—won awards at the North Carolina Brewers Cup.[242] One element of the Kickstarter rewards that has remained in place is the Four Saints Mug Club. Four Saints had local potters create mugs as a patron reward; the mugs were then proudly displayed behind the bar until the mug owner came in to use it. The tradition continues with an annual mug auction that spotlights local potters and raises funds to benefit local charities such as the Randolph County Honor Guard and Our Daily Bread Soup Kitchen.[243]

During this time, growth was not only in the number of craft breweries in operation but in the scale of brewing. The three longest-operating breweries in the region—Red Oak , Natty Greene's and Foothills —all expanded their physical space, providing additional room for production and for customers. Red Oak moved its brewing operations to a new, larger facility in Whitsett in April 2007. The twenty-one tanks that had been in operation at Red Oak's original site moved to the Whitsett facility, and fourteen more were added. A state-of-the-art computerized control room allowed brewmaster Chris Buckley to oversee the operation. The $5 million facility, however, focused solely on brewing. There was no restaurant or taproom for on-site consumption.[244] That changed in December 2017 with the opening of Red Oak's Lager Haus and BierGarten, built as an expansion to the brewing facility and as part of a long-term twenty-eight-thousand-square-foot addition to the site. The six-thousand-square-foot space featured high ceilings and carved wood, with a long bar and large community tables. The two-thousand-square-foot outdoor biergarten showcased landscaping and water features.[245]

Natty Greene's first expanded its space in 2008 with the opening of a production facility on Gate City Boulevard near the Greensboro Coliseum.

People enjoy the expansive outdoor BierGarten at Red Oak Brewery in Whitsett. *Red Oak Brewery.*

Like Red Oak's facility at the time, the production facility was focused solely on brewing operations. There was no taproom or restaurant. Then, in 2017, Natty Greene's founders and co-owners Kayne Fisher and Chris Lester opened Natty Greene's Kitchen + Market at Revolution Mill in Greensboro. The Kitchen + Market, built inside what had once been the carpentry studio for a prominent Greensboro cotton mill, featured a restaurant with multiple Natty Greene's beers on tap as well as a market selling meats, cheeses and other locally sourced goods.[246] In 2018, however, the two business partners split, with Lester keeping Natty Greene's and Fisher becoming the sole owner of the Revolution Mill restaurant, which he renamed Kau. In 2019, Lester expanded Natty Greene's by adding the Brewhouse, a tasting room, to the production facility on Gate City Boulevard.[247]

In Winston-Salem, Foothills also grew its physical space and brewing capacity when it opened a new production facility on Kimwell Road in 2011. In April 2015, Foothills added the twenty-eight-tap Tasting Room to the Kimwell location, offering drinkers an opportunity to gather and sample an array of Foothills beers outside of a restaurant setting. Foothills even expanded its reach beyond craft beer, partnering with local nonprofit organization Bookmarks in 2017 to open Footnote, a café with fresh roasted coffee, cocktails and craft beer within an independent bookshop located next door to the original Foothills location in downtown Winston-Salem.

Expansions and new taproom openings at Red Oak, Natty Greene's and Foothills were accompanied by the opening and growth of many other craft breweries in the region. For instance, in the Lower Fisher Park neighborhood of Greensboro, just north of downtown, Joymongers Brewing Company opened its doors in July 2016. Unlike some of the more established breweries in the region, Joymongers (and many of the other craft breweries that opened during this time) focused largely on bringing people to the taproom to enjoy their beer. Producing beer with an eye toward distribution was not the primary goal. With a frequently rotating menu of beers, Joymongers emphasized variety and showcased many lesser-known styles. Plans to expand Joymongers's reach began in 2017, and in March 2018, the new Joymongers Barrel Hall opened in the West End of Winston-Salem in a former CrossFit gym. While the brewing operations continued at their Greensboro site, the Winston-Salem location focused on aging those beers in oak fermenters. Both locations, however, focused on bringing customers to the taproom by offering a rotating array of beers and beer styles.[248]

Both the established and the newly opened craft breweries throughout the region served (and continue to serve) as gathering places and hosts

Opposite, top: Post-ACC Tournament celebrations at the Natty Greene's Gate City Boulevard location in Greensboro. *Natty Greene's Brewing Co.*

Opposite, bottom: Foothills Brewing Co. Brewery and Tasting Room on Kimwell Drive in Winston-Salem. *Well Crafted NC.*

Above: Joymongers Brewing Co. taproom in Greensboro. *Well Crafted NC.*

for community-focused events that raised money for nonprofits and other charity organizations. Foothills, for instance, launched its Craft Happiness project, which both allows the brewer to create a new monthly IPA using experimental hops and provides financial support and awareness for local nonprofits. Fiddlin' Fish Brewing Company in Winston-Salem partners with Stepping Stones Canine Rescue to provide a highly visible space for adoption events. Nicole Preyer, co-owner of Preyer Brewing Company in Greensboro, summarized the role that many of these craft breweries play in their local communities:

> *It's a place where you can go and make new friends or hang out with new friends or old friends, but you're not having to clean your house. You're not having to have someone over who you might not be ready to take that step yet.*

It's a safe but familiar and comforting place where you can see and hang out with people and be in the public eye without feeling like you're at a baseball game or there's a ton of people around you. You're kind of in your home away from home, and that's really important to us.[249]

2020: COVID-19 and Triad Beer

As it was for most businesses, the year 2020 was tough on the Triad craft brewing industry. In February 2020, two local breweries—Preyer Brewing in Greensboro and Liberty Brewery in High Point—closed their doors. But the COVID-19 pandemic-related closings and the resulting economic downturn that began in March affected large and small breweries across the region. Breweries struggled when health restrictions first closed and then severely limited their taproom attendance. Some had to quickly pivot their business model from one focused on on-site sales in a taproom to one focused only on sales for off-site consumption. And unfortunately, some breweries simply had to cease operations all together, bringing a halt to the period of tremendous growth that the industry saw in the late 2010s.

On March 17, 2020, Governor Roy Cooper signed Executive Order 118, officially closing all restaurants and bars to in-house service. This order forced craft breweries across the state to close their taproom operations to on-site consumption in an effort to stem the spread of the novel coronavirus that had begun to sweep across the nation. During this "Phase 1" period of the state's response to COVID-19, many breweries shifted to a "to go" model by canning their beer or allowing customers to bring in growlers to fill and consume outside of the taproom.[250] But this new model proved particularly challenging for smaller and newer breweries that relied heavily on their taproom and its "community" environment for beer sales.

In Lexington, Goose and the Monkey Brewhouse, the city's first craft brewery, opened its doors on March 1, 2020. The brewery had been in planning for three years, with owners Brent and Ashlee Moore securing a ten-thousand-square-foot space in Lexington's Depot District, a space that had previously housed warehouses for the furniture industry. A large fire in the adjacent Lexington Home Brands Plant 1 building in December 2017 nearly destroyed the future brewery space, with firefighters stopping the blaze right at their door. Construction on the brewery was delayed as the city conducted demolition and clean-up work in the area. Then,

Preyer Brewing Co. in Greensboro. *Erik Lars Myers.*

after only sixteen days in operation, Goose and the Monkey was forced to close its taproom due to Phase 1 restrictions. To continue getting beer into customers' hands, the owners quickly contacted a local mobile canning company, canning fifty cases of the four beers that had been produced for their opening. They set up a temporary sales area outside of the taproom and sold beer to go.[251]

In addition to adapting their service models for pick up only, some local breweries began a delivery service, allowing customers to have cans and growlers of craft beer delivered to their doorsteps. In Winston-Salem, Hoots Beer Company began a delivery service in late March. Customers within a five-mile radius of the brewery could place an order via text or social media and have it delivered the same day. Little Brother Brewing in Greensboro offered a similar service and added both a beer subscription service and a "beergram" service, which allowed customers to order a four-pack of beer to be delivered to a friend's home.[252]

When the state shifted to Phase 2 in late May, brewery taprooms were officially allowed to reopen, but under strict regulations that limited the number of people allowed in the taproom and required social distancing. Canning and delivery options remained available in most cases, but strict guidelines were put in place to ensure craft brewery taprooms were as safe

Left: The Goose and the Monkey Brewhouse, Lexington's first craft beer brewery. *Well Crafted NC.*

Below: Little Brother Brewing Co. on Elm Street in Greensboro. The company resides in the former home of the J.R. Stewart Saloon. *Little Brother Brewing Co.*

COVID-19 messaging and imagery provided to NC breweries by the NC Craft Brewers Guild. *North Carolina Craft Brewers Guild.*

as possible. The North Carolina Craft Brewers Guild developed an "NC Beer Brewery Pledge," asking members to prominently display a copy of the statement indicating "the industry's commitment to the health and safety of our communities and employees." The pledge included promises that high-touch and high-traffic areas would be cleaned and sanitized frequently, that hand washing and sanitizing stations would be available for customers, that social distancing and face mask guidelines would be in place and that all staff would pass a health check prior to the start of their work shifts. A similar "NC Beer Consumer Pledge" outlined the regulations and expectations for customers.[253]

Craft breweries with sizable outdoor spaces adapted by creating new seating areas to expand their capacity for on-site service even when the taproom numbers were necessarily cut. For instance, Oden Brewing Company opened in Greensboro in November 2019. Located on Gate City Boulevard near the University of North Carolina at Greensboro, the brewery's large taproom quickly became a gathering place for the campus community and others in Greensboro. When the state moved into Phase 2 and the taprooms could reopen for on-site consumption, Oden took advantage of the large open lawn outside of the brewery building and added a series of picnic tables, spaced at least six feet apart. Additionally, it operated a service window from the patio that allowed patrons to order their beer without having to come inside the building.

#NCBeer Pledge

The #NCBeer Pledge is our commitment to our customers.
We have taken the Pledge so you know we are in compliance with COVID-19 recommended safety guidelines and are doing our part to protect the safety of our community.

Our Pledge to YOU:

- We will continue to be a leader in sanitation and food safety.
- All high-touch surfaces are regularly cleaned & sanitized.
- Seating areas are cleaned & sanitized between customers.
- Indoor and/or outdoor seating complies with recommended social-distancing guidance.
- Hand washing or sanitizing stations are made available to you .
- All staff will pass a health check prior to each shift.
- Glassware & utensils are sanitized after each use.
- Common areas and restrooms are cleaned & sanitized regularly.
- All staff will maintain 6 feet of social distance when possible, or will wear a face covering or use a guard/barrier when not possible.
- We have a designated Safety & Sanitation Manager on-site to oversee safety and sanitation measures, as well as address any concerns.

The North Carolina Craft Brewers Guild ☀ www.ncbeer.org ☀ promotions@ncbeer.org

This page and opposite: COVID-19 brewery #NCBeer Pledge material for display in taprooms. *North Carolina Craft Brewers Guild.*

#NCBeer Pledge

The #NCBeer Pledge is your commitment to the community.
We are asking our customers to take the Pledge for the safety of our staff, friends, and neighbors. We all have a role to play in protecting the common good.

Your Pledge to US:
- You will maintain 6 feet of physical distance between yourself and other customers.
- You will wear a mask or face covering when not seated, or when waiting in line.
- You will not congregate while standing, nor float between tables.
- No large parties, unless of the same family and household.

| **WEAR** | **WAIT** | **WASH** |
| a cloth face covering. | 6 feet apart and avoid close contact. | your hands often or use hand sanitizer |

If you are experiencing any symptoms of, or have recently been exposed to, COVID-19, please use our to-go pickup options.

 The North Carolina Craft Brewers Guild * www.ncbeer.org * promotions@ncbeer.org

Unfortunately, not all local craft breweries were able to survive the economic impact of the pandemic. Gibb's Hundred Brewing Company opened in downtown Greensboro in 2014 after owner Mark Gibb led the movement to redefine *brewpub* and *brewery* to allow microbreweries with taprooms to open in the main business district. The following year, Gibb's Hundred won a gold medal at the Great American Beer Festival for its

During the COVID-19 pandemic, social distancing and masking were apparent at the Red Oak Lager Haus in Whitsett. *Red Oak Brewery.*

"Guilty Party" Extra Special Bitter (ESB). In 2017, Gibb purchased an 8,600-square-foot building in the State Street area of Greensboro, and Gibb's Hundred left its downtown space. The new State Street location featured a spacious taproom, an outdoor beer garden and a large production space. Gibb's Hundred had developed into the seventh-largest brewer in the area by volume produced, but the COVID-19 pandemic exacerbated other financial issues.[254] On September 13, Gibb's Hundred closed its doors. In the announcement of the closing, Gibb noted, "We've struggled to stay afloat during the pandemic, but it's proved to be too much."[255]

The pandemic also damaged one of Greensboro's original breweries, Natty Greene's. In November 2019, Natty Greene's announced a plan for $800,000 in renovations to its Elm Street brewpub.[256] Those renovations were completed in March 2020, just in time for the pandemic-related closing mandate. March would have also brought a large crowd to both Elm Street and the Brewhouse location near the Greensboro Coliseum, as Greensboro was set to host the Atlantic Coast Conference men's basketball championship. The tournament, however, was initially limited to essential personnel and select guests only then canceled all together on the third day of play.[257] The Brewhouse location announced that it would close indefinitely on October 8,

Owner Mark Gibb in the Gibb's Hundred Brewing Co. taproom on Lewis Street. *Gibb's Hundred Brewing Co.*

Gibb's Hundred Brewing Co. Lewis Street taproom. *Gibb's Hundred Brewing Co.*

specifically citing the pandemic as its reason for closure.[258] Later that month, the corporation that owned the brewery portion of Natty Greene's filed for Chapter 7 bankruptcy protection. The brewing portion of the business and all its assets were turned over to the courts to help settle the $5.8 million debt that Natty Greene's owned to creditors.[259]

Natty Greene's beers, however, did not disappear thanks to a partnership formed with SouthEnd Brewing Company. SouthEnd opened in late October 2019 in the downtown Greensboro location previously occupied by Gibb's Hundred. Head Brewer William Brown had deep roots in the Triad beer scene, previously working at Gibb's Hundred and at Burlington Beer Works. When Natty Greene's filed for bankruptcy and lost its brewing equipment, SouthEnd stepped up. Working with the SouthEnd team, Natty Greene's was able to brew and keg beers at the SouthEnd facility, allowing continued sales of Buckshot Amber and other Natty Greene's staples at the Elm Street restaurant.[260]

The Natty Greene's brewpub as seen from the Little Brother Brewing Co. taproom on Elm Street in downtown Greensboro. *Well Crafted NC.*

The Triad craft beer scene has changed dramatically since 2014, and at the beginning of 2021, it is difficult to predict what it will look like in five months, much less in five years. A full list of Triad craft breweries in operation at the start of 2021 is available in the appendix. You will find their locations and contact information as well as a brief history of each brewery. These craft breweries are part of a long tradition in the region that dates to the Moravian brewers in the Bethabara community in the late 1700s. As these businesses continue their work in an uncertain future, they continue to demonstrate a sense of professional camaraderie and collaboration that will hopefully help them continue to grow in years to come.

TRIAD CRAFT BREWERIES TODAY

Creating a definitive list of craft breweries in operation at any point in time is difficult. Breweries open and close. Some that are currently in planning are scheduled to open soon, but some may never come to be. It is particularly challenging to create this type of list at the start of 2021, when COVID-19 is still forcing operational changes and the long-term economic impact of the pandemic is yet to be seen.

The brewhouse at Haw River Farmhouse Ales in Saxapahaw. *Erik Lars Myers.*

What we have chosen to do here is list all the craft breweries with open taprooms in the Triad region as of January 1, 2021. This list does not include breweries that may have closed temporarily due to the pandemic, breweries in planning or breweries that do not operate a public taproom. Each brewery is listed with its location, web address and a brief history.

Craft breweries in the Triad are sources for economic revitalization, reuse of industrial spaces and community activity and engagement. We hope that there will be many new additions (and no subtractions) to this list over the coming years.

ALAMANCE COUNTY

Bright Penny Brewing

107 North Seventh Street
Mebane, NC 27302
www.orderbrightpennybrewing.com/

Co-owners Jeremy and Christina Carroll and Jason Brand opened Bright Penny Brewing in Mebane in May 2019. A fall 2018 Kickstarter campaign provided the funds to purchase the five fermenters in place at opening. The brewery is located in Mebane's former Rice Flour and Feed Mill building.

Burlington Beer Works

103 East Front Street
Burlington, NC 27215
www.burlingtonbeerworks.coop

Burlington Beer Works opened in late March 2019 as Burlington's first brewery and North Carolina's first cooperatively owned brewpub. Individuals could purchase a share of the brewery for $100. The brewery actively collaborates with the East of Elon Home Brewing Cooperative and other local homebrewing groups on recipes and ingredient sourcing.

Forgotten Road Ales

141 East Harden Street
Graham, NC 27253
www.facebook.com/forgottenroadales/

Owners Ben and Janee Farrar opened Forgotten Road Ales, Graham's first craft brewery, in May 2019. The brewery, located in downtown Graham, specializes in barrel-aged beers, wild and sour beers and hazy IPAs. The name of the brewery is a nod to military veterans, with the branding and logo design based on Ben's final rank of staff sergeant in the Marines.

Haw River Farmhouse Ales

1713 Saxapahaw-Bethlehem Church Road
Saxapahaw, NC 27340
www.hawriverales.com

Haw River Farmhouse Ales was opened by owner Ben Woodward in 2014 in the former Dixie Yarns mechanical room in Saxapahaw. Haw River specializes in Belgian-inspired farmhouse ales and incorporates locally grown ingredients. Its Farmhand Exchange program provides local growers with a packet of vegetable seeds that, when harvested, the brewery will buy back at market value and use in a new beer. In 2019, Haw River was the fifth-largest brewery in the Triad region, producing approximately 1,800 barrels.

Toasty Kettlyst Beer Company

106 West Main Street
Gibsonville, NC 27249
www.toastykettlyst.com

Downtown Gibsonville got its first craft brewery in November 2020 when Toasty Kettlyst opened on Main Street. Owner Praveen Karandikar had a background in homebrewing before opening the nanobrewery, which features a three-and-a-half-barrel system.

DAVIDSON COUNTY

Goose and the Monkey Brewhouse

401 South Railroad Street
Lexington, NC 27292
www.gooseandthemonkeybrewhouse.com

Goose and the Monkey Brewhouse was in planning by owners Brent and Ashlee Moore for many years before it officially opened in March 2020 as Lexington's first craft brewery. After securing a ten-thousand-square-foot location in 2017, construction plans were halted after a massive fire swept through Lexington's Depot District, stopping right at the brewery's building. It took three years of clean-up and construction before Goose and the Monkey could open. Then sixteen days after opening, the taproom was closed due to COVID-19. The brewery adapted by quickly developing its outdoor seating and working with a local mobile canning service to prepare beers for off-site consumption.

FORSYTH COUNTY

Fiddlin' Fish Brewing Company

772 Trade Street NW
Winston-Salem, NC 27101
www.fiddlinfish.com

Fiddlin' Fish Brewing Company opened in 2017 as Winston-Salem's fifth craft brewery. Owners Dave Ashe and Stuart Barnhart adapted a former tobacco warehouse on Trade Street for their taproom and fifteen-barrel production space. Their love of fishing and bluegrass music led to the

brewery's name. Fiddlin' Fish typically offers fourteen beers on tap, with one of the most popular being "That Fish Cray New England IPA."

Fiddlin' Fish Brewing Co. on Trade Street NW in downtown Winston-Salem. *Fiddlin' Fish Brewing Co.*

Foothills Brewing Company

www.foothillsbrewing.com
Three locations:

Downtown Brewpub
638 West Fourth Street
Winston-Salem, NC 27101

Footnote
634 West Fourth Street
Suite 120
Winston-Salem, NC 27101

Tasting Room
3800 Kimwell Drive
Winston-Salem, NC 27103

Foothills opened in 2005 as Winston-Salem's first craft brewery. Owner Jamie Bartholomaus served as the head brewer until 2010, when T.L. Adkisson was hired. Foothills expanded its production space in 2011 with a new facility on Kimwell Road. A tasting room was added to that building in 2015. Further growth came in 2017 when they opened Footnote, a café with fresh roasted coffee, cocktails and craft beer within an independent bookshop located next door to the original brewpub location in downtown Winston-Salem. In 2019, Foothills ranked as the Triad region's top craft brewery by production.

The Foothills Brewing taproom on Kimwell Drive in Winston-Salem. *Well Crafted NC.*

Gypsy Road Brewing Company

1105 East Mountain Street
Kernersville, NC 27284
www.gypsyroadbrewing.com

Gypsy Road Brewing Company opened a taproom in September 2018, selling beer brewed by other businesses. In 2019, owners John and Tammy Coulter and Taylor Thornton along with brewer Adam Norman officially began offering their own house-made beer on tap—Wit My Whistle Watermelon Wheat, Hazy IPA and Macy Grove Pale Ale. As the number of house-made beers grew, Gypsy Road phased out most of its guest taps and focused on its own brews.

Hoots Beer Company

840 Mill Works Street
Winston-Salem, NC 27101
www.hootspublic.com

The Hoots Roller Mill, constructed in the 1930s for flour milling, is now home to Hoots Roller Bar and Beer Company. Hoots opened its doors in 2013 as a bar but quickly added a brewing system for producing its own craft beer. Eric Swaim, Eric Weyer and Ralph Pritts are the founders and co-owners of Hoots, which continues to serve craft cocktails alongside house-made beer at their location in Winston-Salem's West End.

Hoots Roller Bar in Winston-Salem. *Erik Lars Myers.*

Incendiary Brewing Company

486 North Patterson Avenue
Winston-Salem, NC 27101
www.incendiarybrewing.com

On Labor Day weekend 2019, owners Brandon Branscome and John Bacon opened Incendiary Brewing Company on the first floor of Winston-Salem's Bailey Power Plant, a building that had formerly provided power to the bustling R.J. Reynolds Tobacco Company factory. John Priest, formerly of Gibb's Hundred in Greensboro, served as the first head brewer. In 2016, as homebrewers, Branscome and Bacon won gold at the Master's Championship of Amateur Brewing for their Shift IPA, and Incendiary's beer menu reflects their love of IPAs through their Shift series.

Kernersville Brewing Company

210 North Main Street
Kernersville, NC 27284
www.kernersvillebrewing.com

Kernersville Brewing Company, the first craft brewery in Kernersville, dates to January 2016 when founder Dwight Deal started brewing and selling beer wholesale from a 350-square-foot space on North Main Street. In January 2019, KBS opened a 3,000-square-foot taproom. To meet the growing demand for its beer, KBS also expanded to include a production facility on East Mountain Street, increasing capacity from fifty-five barrels to at least five hundred barrels per year.

Radar Brewing Company

216 East Ninth Street
Winston-Salem, NC 27101
www.radarbrewingcompany.com

Radar Brewing Company opened on Ninth Street in Winston-Salem's Industry Hill area on New Year's Day 2020. Radar's beers are brewed through an open fermentation process, with the brewery housing a ten-by-ten-foot open fermentation room. Radar's co-founders all have strong ties in the Triad's craft beer industry. Co-founders Aaron Wall and Aaron Sizemore both attended the brewing, fermentation and distilling program at Rockingham Community College, and both worked at Natty Greene's in Greensboro. The third co-founder, Eric Peck, previously worked at Foothills in Winston-Salem. (Wall had also worked at Foothills.)

Small Batch Beer Company

241 West Fifth Street
Winston-Salem, NC 27101
www.smallbatchws.com

Small Batch Beer Company opened in Winston-Salem's West Fifth Street area in 2014. Founders Ryan Blain, Cliff Etscason and Tim Walker selected the name to match the nanobrewery's intent—to produce smaller batches and allow for experimentation. In 2016, the business expanded with the opening of Burger Batch restaurant next door. A second Burger Batch restaurant opened in High Point in 2018.

Westbend Winery and Brewery

5394 Williams Road
Lewisville, NC 27023
www.westbendwineryandbrewery.com

Westbend Winery opened in 1972 in the Yadkin Valley. Beer brewing was first added in 2012, but in 2014, the original owner was forced to close the winery, brewery and tasting room. In 2014, the business was sold to Walt and Sonia Breathwit. They and their son Ryan Blinkhorn reopened the business, including the brewery and newly constructed tasting room, in December 2016.

Wise Man Brewing Company

826 Angelo Brothers Avenue
Winston-Salem, NC 27101
www.wisemanbrewing.com

Wise Man Brewing Company opened its doors in January 2017 in the ninety-year-old former Angelos Brothers Wholesale building. By 2019, it had grown to be the fourth-largest craft brewery by production in the Triad. That same year, Wise Man was named a Top Ten brewery and received four medals in the U.S. Open Beer Championship. It also claimed gold in the Irish-Style Red Ale category at the 2019 Great American Beer Festival for its Outrageous Daughters ale.

Wise Man Brewing Co. in Winston-Salem, housed in a 1929 warehouse and former Angelo Bros. Wholesale location. *Well Crafted NC.*

GUILFORD COUNTY

Brown Truck Brewery

1234 North Main Street
High Point, NC 27262
www.browntruckbrewery.com

Owners John and Kelly Vaughan and Britt and Sarah Lytle opened Brown Truck Brewery in High Point in 2016 and quickly began to earn accolades for their beer. At the 2016 Great American Beer Festival, Brown Truck won the award for Very Small Brewing Company of the Year. It also won a gold medal in the American Light Lager category and silvers in both the Saison and Dry-Hopped Saison categories.

Goofy Foot Brewery

2762 NC-68
Suite 109
High Point, NC 27265
www.goofyfoottaproom.com

Goofy Foot Taproom opened in Heron Village in High Point in 2018. While
Goofy Foot primarily serves as a bottle shop and tasting room focused on
North Carolina beer, owner Jeff Thompson also sells house-brewed beers
created in thirty-gallon batches on a single-barrel brew system.

Joymongers Brewing Company

www.joymongers.com

Two locations:
Greensboro   *Barrel Hall* (Forsyth County)
576 N Eugene St.   480 West End Blvd.
Greensboro, NC 27401   Winston-Salem, NC 27101

Jim Jones, Brian Jones and Mike Rollinson opened Joymongers Brewing
Company in the Lower Fisher Park neighborhood of Greensboro just north
of downtown in July 2016. Rollinson serves as head brewer, focusing on a
rotating menu of small-batch beers. In March 2018, the new Joymongers
Barrel Hall opened in the West End of Winston-Salem in a former CrossFit
gym. While the brewing operations continued at the Greensboro site, the
Winston-Salem location focused on aging those beers in oak fermenters.

Leveneleven Brewing

1111 Coliseum Boulevard
Greensboro, NC 27403
www.leveneleven.com

Dan Morgan was an avid homebrewer who opened a homebrewing supply
shop—Big Dan's Brew Shed—in Greensboro in the early 2010s. The Brew
Shed moved to a new location in a strip mall across the street from the
Greensboro Coliseum in 2017. In 2018, Morgan opened Leveneleven

Brewing in a 2,200-square-foot space in that same strip mall. Leveneleven operates a three-barrel system, producing both classic styles and more experimental brews.

Little Brother Brewing Company

www.littlebrotherbrew.com

Two locations:

Greensboro
348 South Elm Street
Greensboro, NC 27401

Barrel and Bottle (Alamance County)
106 West Elm Street
Graham, NC 27253

Founders Daniel McCoy and Jeff Collie opened Little Brother Brewing Company in downtown Greensboro, across Elm Street from Natty Greene's, in November 2017. Little Brother won gold at the 2018 Great American Beer festival for their Civil Rest Hefeweizen. The Homebrewer Spotlight program allows local homebrewers to collaborate with head brewer Stephen Monahan and learn how to produce beer on a commercial

system. In November 2020, Little Brother expanded by opening Little Brother Brewing: Barrel and Bottle in Graham.

Holiday decorations at Little Brother Brewing Co. in Greensboro. *Little Brother Brewing Co.*

Natty Greene's Brewing Company

345 South Elm Street
Greensboro, NC 27401
www.nattygreenes.com

Co-owners Kayne Fisher and Chris Lester opened Natty Greene's Brewing Company in August 2004 as Greensboro's second brewpub. They expanded their production space in 2008 with the opening of a facility on Gate City Boulevard, and in 2017, they opened Natty Greene's Kitchen + Market at Revolution Mill. In 2018, however, the two business partners split, with Lester keeping Natty Greene's. In 2019, Lester added the Brewhouse, a tasting room, to the production facility. In October 2020, however, the Brewhouse announced that it would close indefinitely. Later that month, the corporation that owned the brewery portion of Natty Greene's filed for Chapter 7 bankruptcy protection. Natty Greene's continues to brew beer through a partnership with SouthEnd Brewing Company.

Production facility at Natty Greene's brewery. *Natty Greene's Brewing Co.*

Oden Brewing Company

804 West Gate City Boulevard
Greensboro, NC 27403
www.odenbrewing.com

Bill and Jan Oden opened Oden Brewing Company in November 2019 in the former site of a family-owned bottling company. Located on Gate City Boulevard near the UNC Greensboro, Oden Brewing features decorative elements to highlight the building's history and industrial feel. Former Natty Greene's brewer Brian Carter was hired as Oden Brewing's head brewer in 2019.

Pig Pounder Brewery

1107 Grecade Street
Greensboro, NC 27408
www.pigpounder.com

Owner Marty Kotis opened Pig Pounder Brewery in the Midtown area of Greensboro 2014, initially focused on producing beer to supply restaurants he owned in Greensboro. Pig Pounder's beer menu includes many English-style beers, and its Boar Brown won a gold medal in the English Brown Ale category at the 2016 World Beer Cup. An $800,000 expansion to the brewery in 2018 added both a tasting room and added to the production space.

Pig Pounder Brewery
in Greensboro.
Erik Lars Myers.

Red Oak Brewery

6901 Konica Drive
Whitsett, NC 27377
www.redoakbrewery.com

Red Oak originated as Spring Garden Brewing Company in Greensboro 1991. Owned by Bill Sherrill, it is the longest-operating craft brewery in the Triad region. In 2001, the brewery name was changed to Red Oak in honor of one of its most popular brews. Red Oak moved brewing operations to a new, larger facility in Whitsett in April 2007. In December 2017, it opened the Lager Haus and BierGarten, an expansion to the brewing facility that featured a large taproom and outdoor space. Red Oak was the Triad's second-largest brewery by production in 2019.

A view of Interstate 40 over the stainless-steel tanks at Red Oak Brewery in Whitsett. *Red Oak Brewery.*

SouthEnd Brewing Company

117 West Lewis Street
Greensboro, NC 27406
www.southendbrewing.com

SouthEnd Brewing Company opened in Greensboro in October 2019 in a downtown space formerly occupied by Gibb's Hundred Brewing Company. Owners Eric and Seth Kevorkian hired William Brown, previously a brewer at Gibb's, as their head brewer. In addition to renovating the taproom and adding a small kitchen to the space, the SouthEnd team created a beer garden outdoor space in the area that formerly served as a loading dock.

RANDOLPH COUNTY

Four Saints Brewing Company

218 South Fayetteville Street
Asheboro, NC 27203
www.foursaintsbrewing.com

Four Saints Brewing Company was the first brewery to open in Asheboro after the city voted to allow alcohol sales in 2008. Owners Joel McClosky and Andrew Deming had experience homebrewing together, and in 2011,

A four-beer flight ready for sampling at Four Saints in Asheboro. *Erik Lars Myers.*

they began work to open a craft brewery in Asheboro's downtown. After four years of planning and a successful Kickstarter campaign, they opened Four Saints in 2015. The brewery is named after four patron saints of brewing—Luke, Augustine of Hippo, Wenceslaus and Nicholas. Four Saints offers seasonal beers named in tribute to these four, as well as a Devil's Advocate series that introduces pilot batches of new or variant beers.

ROCKINGHAM COUNTY

Hell on Horsecreek Brewing

107 East Murphy Street
Madison, NC 27025
www.hellonhorsecreek.com

In October 2019, Hell on Horsecreek Brewing opened in a former funeral parlor in historic downtown Madison. Owner David Peters had previously worked as a chemical manufacturing engineer, but his love of homebrewing led him to open Hell on Horsecreek. Many of the beers at Hell on Horsecreek feature a play on the theme "Smoke and Fire," including beers with smoked barley and rye or spicy peppers.

SURREY COUNTY

Angry Troll Brewing Company

222 East Main Street
Elkin, NC 28621
www.angrytrollbrewing.com

Angry Troll Brewing Company began as a collaborative venture, with multiple business partners and fundraising through the crowdfunding platform Indiegogo. The brewery opened in 2016 in the lower level of a building that once served as a Liberty Tobacco warehouse on Elkin's Main Street. The name of the brewery is a play on both its location in the building's lower level and as a reminder of the nearby Hugh Chatham Memorial Bridge, a local landmark that was demolished in 2010. In 2017, Angry Troll merged with the restaurant 222 Public House, located on the upper level of the Liberty Building, to open a brewpub that would feature Angry Troll beers.

Midsummer Brewing

8544 NC-89 W
Westfield, NC 27053
www.midsummerbrewing.com

Co-owners Jeff Noethlich, Dwight Hostert and Rich Larsen spent two years building production and getting permits to open Midsummer Brewing, a brewery in an outbuilding on the same property as Noethlich's family home. They began producing beer on a three-barrel system and distributing locally in 2020. On October 17, 2020, Midsummer hosted the official grand opening of its taproom.

Skull Camp Brewing

2000 North Bridge Street
Elkin, NC 28621
www.skullcampbrewing.com

Skull Camp has its roots at the Round Peak Vineyards, which was purchased by owners Kari Heerdt and Ken Gulaian in 2008. Microbrewing was added to the wine operations in mid-2012. By 2014, the beer had proven popular, and a ten-barrel production system was added. In late 2017, the owners opened the Skull Camp Brewery and Smokehouse with a beer and wine tasting room in a renovated general store building on North Bridge Street in Elkin.

Thirsty Souls Community Brewing

238 Market Street
Mount Airy, NC 27030
www.thirstysoulsbrewing.com

Thirsty Souls Community Brewing on Market Street in historic downtown Mount Airy opened in 2017 in the former site of Moody's Funeral Service. Slovakian native Jan Kriska, who co-owns Thirsty Souls with his wife, Maria, serves as the head brewer, focusing primarily on European-style beers.

White Elephant Beer Company

225 Market Street
Mount Airy, NC 27030
www.whiteelephantbeer.com

Driven largely by the interests of founder Todd Butcher and his family, White Elephant Beer Company opened on Market Street in historic downtown Mount Airy in 2016. Originally a bottle shop and taproom, White Elephant began brewing its own beers on a three-barrel system. Kent Yocco serves as co-owner and head brewer. Stouts with adjuncts and juicy IPAs are among the house specialties.

NOTES

Introduction

1. "North Carolina's Craft Beer Sales and Production, 2019," Brewers Association, accessed February 2, 2021, http://www.brewersassociation.org/statistics-and-data/state-craft-beer-stats/?state=NC.

1. Beer and Brewing in Early North Carolina

2. John Brickell, *The Natural History of North Carolina* (Dublin: James Carson, 1737), 38.
3. Robert M. Dunkerly, *Redcoats on the Cape Fear: The Revolutionary War in Southeastern North Carolina*, revised edition (Jefferson, NC: McFarland, 2014), 7.
4. Franklin Tursi, *Winston-Salem: A History* (Winston-Salem, NC: J.F. Blair, 1994), 37.
5. Tursi, *Winston-Salem*, 27–34.
6. Adelaide L. Fries, ed., *Records of the Moravians in North Carolina* [hereafter *Records*], vol. 1, *1752–1771* (Raleigh, NC: Edwards and Broughton, 1922), 247.
7. *Records*, vol. 1, 160.
8. *Records*, vol. 1, 287.
9. *Records*, vol. 1, 359.

10. Stanley South, *Historical Archaeology in Wachovia: Excavating Eighteenth-Century Bethabara and Moravian Pottery* (New York: Kluwer Academic/ Plenum Publishers, 205), 71–77.

11. *Records*, vol. 1, 392.

12. *Records*, vol. 1, 354.

13. Adelaide L. Fries, ed., *Records of the Moravians in North Carolina*, vol. 6, *1793– 1808* (Raleigh: North Carolina Historical Commission, 1943), 2716.

14. *Records*, vol. 6, 2752.

15. *Records*, vol. 6, 2886.

16. Tursi, *Winston-Salem*, 50.

17. Adelaide L. Fries, ed., *Records of the Moravians in North Carolina*, vol. 2, *1752 –1775* (Raleigh, NC: Edwards and Broughton, 1925), 697.

18. David Rice, "Moravians: Let There Be Beer, Trials of an Early Brewery," *Winston-Salem Journal*, September 5, 1993.

19. Jerry L. Surratt, "Salem Tavern," *NCpedia*, accessed February 2, 2021, http://www.ncpedia.org/salem-tavern.

20. *Records*, vol. 6, 2820, 3142, 3254.

21. "Town of Salem: 1793–1803," City of Winston-Salem, accessed February 2, 2021, http://www.cityofws.org/DocumentCenter/View/2816/Salem-1793-to-1803-PDF.

22. Surratt, "Salem Tavern."

2. Saloons of the Triad

23. "Oyster Saloon," *Greensboro Patriot*, December 22, 1870.

24. Bethuel Merritt Newcomb, *Andrew Newcomb, 1618–1686, and His Descendants* (United States: Privately printed for the author by the Tuttle, Morehouse & Taylor Company, 1923), 350.

25. *Greensboro Patriot*, April 2, 1873; "New Grocery," *Greensboro Patriot*, May 12, 1875.

26. "McAdoo Hotel Ruined, the C.W. Gold Residence Destroyed, and Two Other Homes Damaged by Flames Thursday," *Greensboro Daily News*, May 12, 1916.

27. "A Famous Saloonist," *Reidsville Review*, November 5, 1897.

28. "The Newcomb Case," *Greensboro Evening Telegram*, December 9, 1899.

29. Newcomb, *Andrew Newcomb*, 350.

30. Unless otherwise noted, all specific address listings from 1884 through 1910 are culled from listings in the Greensboro and Winston-Salem city directories.

31. "Samuel Johnson McCauley," FindAGrave.com, accessed February 2, 2021, https://www.findagrave.com/memorial/28282755/samuel-johnson-mccauley.
32. "Destructive Fire," *Greensboro Patriot*, June 11, 1891; *Greensboro Patriot*, August 7, 1895.
33. "Refilled the Tank," *Greensboro Telegram*, May 30, 1898; "Compelled to Close," *Greensboro Telegram*, February 7, 1899.
34. Susan Ladd, "Cascade Saloon Holds a Mystery of Greensboro History," *Greensboro News and Record*, February 11, 2017.
35. "Completion of Cascade Saloon Redevelopment Celebrated," Christman Company, June 14, 2018, https://www.christmanco.com/Company/News/completion-of-cascade-saloon-redevelopment-celebrated.
36. "Local News Items," *Greensboro Patriot*, December 7, 1898.
37. "The Dispensary Abolished," *Greensboro Patriot*, January 16, 1901. Note that Shoffner's saloon building served as the site of the dispensary during its year and a half of operation.
38. "Dissolution Notice," *Greensboro Patriot*, August 6, 1902.
39. "Shoffner Buys Property," *Winston-Salem Journal*, December 15, 1906.
40. From Winston-Salem city directories published from 1879 to 1910.
41. From Winston-Salem city directories published from 1896 to 1906.
42. "Mr. J.W Warren Hurt," *Western Sentinel*, September 14, 1906.
43. "Found Brother Strangely Slain," *Greensboro Daily News*, January 23, 1906.
44. "Who Killed Henry Kobre?," *Union Republican* (Winston-Salem, NC), January 25, 1906.
45. "Mrs. Kitty Baldwin Gave Wonderful Occult Performance at Grand Last Night," *Greensboro Daily News*, February 16, 1906.
46. "Two Arrested for the Kobre Murder," *Greensboro Daily News*, March 6, 1906; "What Shouse Knew," *Winston-Salem Journal*, March 7, 1906.
47. "Examination of Witnesses in Kobre Murder Trial Brings to Light Many Interesting, Revelations," *Winston-Salem Journal*, May 30, 1906; "Three Defendants in Murder Trial Give Testimony," *Winston-Salem Journal*, May 31, 1906; "The Defendants Are Acquitted," *Winston-Salem Journal*, June 1, 1906.
48. "Examination of Witnesses"; "Three Defendants in Murder Trial"; "Defendants Are Acquitted."
49. "Society," *Winston-Salem Journal*, June 22, 1910.
50. "Strychnine Is Fatal to Sam Kobre," *Bee* (Danville, VA), December 15, 1933.
51. "Notes of Interest," *Winston-Salem Journal*, February 13, 1909.

52. "Greensboro Keeps Busy Saloons of Reidsville," *Greensboro Daily News*, May 23, 1906.

53. Advertisement, *Danbury Reporter*, September 20, 1906.

54. Advertisement, *Reidsville Review*, February 28, 1889.

55. Advertisement, *Reidsville Review*, January 25, 1895; Advertisement, *Reidsville Review*, May 27, 1891.

56. Advertisement, *Reidsville Review*, March 5, 1901; *Reidsville Review*, December 31, 1901.

57. Advertisement, *Reidsville Review*, March 19, 1890; Advertisement, *Reidsville Review*, May 27, 1891.

58. *Danbury Reporter*, May 31, 1906. Sheets also operated a distillery in Danbury.

3. Prohibition in the Triad

59. "Acts of the North Carolina General Assembly, 1715–1716," *Colonial and State Records of North Carolina*. From Documenting the American South, accessed February 2, 2021, http://docsouth.unc.edu/csr/index.php/document/csr23-0001.

60. Hance McCain, "To the Friends of Morality," *Hillsborough Recorder*, June 12, 1822.

61. *People's Press*, May 25, 1855.

62. "Town of Winston Directing Board: 1849–1869," City of Winston-Salem, accessed May 25, 2020, https://www.cityofws.org/DocumentCenter/View/2834/Winston-1849-to-1869-PDF

63. "Town of Winston Directing Board: 1870–1879," City of Winston-Salem, accessed May 25, 2020, https://www.cityofws.org/DocumentCenter/View/2833/Winston-1870-to-1879-PDF

64. Joseph M. Reece, "Here and Hereabouts," *Greensboro North State*, May 5, 1876.

65. Advertisement, *Greensboro North State*, September 29, 1876.

66. *Carolina Watchman*, May 26, 1881.

67. "Temperance Notes," *Greensboro North State*, August 9, 1883.

68. Edward Rondthaler, *The Memorabilia of Fifty Years, 1877 to 1927* (Raleigh, NC: Edwards & Broughton Company, 1928), 72.

69. "The Prohibition Party," *Weekly State Chronicle*, December 17, 1885.

70. "An Act to Prohibit the Manufacture and Sale of Spirituous and Malt Liquors," *Laws and Resolutions of the State of North Carolina, Passed by the General*

Assembly at Its Session [1881], ch. 319, 554, accessed February 2, 2021, http://digital.ncdcr.gov/digital/collection/p249901coll22/id/198421.

71. R.D.W. Connor, *A Manual of North Carolina* (Raleigh: North Carolina Historical Commission, 1913), 1019–20, accessed February 2, 2021, http://archive.org/details/manualofnorthcar1913nort/page/1018/mode/2up.

72. "The Scene of Battle," *Greensboro Telegram*, February 17, 1899.

73. *Greensboro Patriot*, June 28, 1899.

74. "Local News Items," *Greensboro Patriot*, July 26, 1899.

75. A.W. McAllister, "The Facts in the Case," *Greensboro Telegram*, August 26, 1899.

76. "Paid to Quit," *Greensboro Telegram*, August 17, 1899.

77. "The Dispensary Stands," *Greensboro Telegram*, March 14, 1900.

78. Editorials, *Greensboro Telegram*, June 9, 1900.

79. "The Dispensary Must Go," *Greensboro Telegram*, August 3, 1900.

80. Daniel J. Whitener, *Prohibition in North Carolina, 1715–1945* (Chapel Hill: University of North Carolina Press, 1946), 53.

81. "Greensboro Keeps Busy Saloons of Reidsville," *Greensboro Daily News*, May 23, 1906, Newspapers.com.

82. "An Act to Regulate the Manufacture and Sale of Liquors in North Carolina," *Public Laws and Resolutions of the State of North Carolina Passed by the General Assembly at Its Session [1903]*, ch. 233, 288, accessed February 2, 2021, http://digital.ncdcr.gov/digital/collection/p249901coll22/id/230699/rec/1.

83. "An Act to Amend Chapter 233 Of the Public Laws of 1903, Regulating the Manufacture and Sale of Liquors in North Carolina," *Public Laws and Resolutions of the State of North Carolina Passed by the General Assembly at Its session [1905]*, ch. 339, 360, accessed February 2, 2021, http://digital.ncdcr.gov/digital/collection/p249901coll22/id/232196/rec/1.

84. L. Stott Blakey, *The Sale of Liquor in the South: The History of the Development of a Normal Social Restraint in Southern Commonwealths* (New York, 1912), 34.

85. "Carrie Nation," *Hickory Democrat*, August 1, 1907.

86. "Carrie Nation Does Salisbury Brown," *Monroe Journal*, July 02, 1907.

87. "Local News," *Greensboro Patriot*, July 24, 1907.

88. "An Act to Prohibit the Manufacture and Sale of Intoxicating Liquors in North Carolina," *Public Laws and Resolutions of the State of North Carolina Passed by the General Assembly at Its Session [1908]*, ch. 71, 83–87, accessed February 2, 2021, http://digital.ncdcr.gov/digital/collection/p249901coll22/id/223867.

89. National Association of Distillers and Wholesale Dealers, *The Anti-Prohibition Manual: A Summary of Facts and Figures Dealing with Prohibition* (Cincinnati: National Association of Distillers and Wholesale Dealers, 1917), 8, accessed February 2, 2021, http://archive.org/details/antiprohibitionm17nati/page/8/mode/2up.

90. Connor, *A Manual of North Carolina*, 1019–20.

91. Connor, *Manual of North Carolina*, 1019–20.

92. "Winston-Salem News," *Greensboro Daily News*, January 7, 1909.

93. *Winston-Salem Journal*, December 7, 1909.

94. "Blind Tigers Are Busy," *Greensboro Daily News*, July 24, 1910.

95. "Prohibition Made a Farce in Lexington," *Greensboro Patriot*, August 17, 1910.

96. "Held for Higher Court," *Greensboro Patriot*, June 22, 1910.

97. "House Destroyed by Dynamite Bomb," *Winston Salem Journal*, June 12, 1910.

98. "Held for Higher Court."

99. "Destroyed by Dynamite," *Greensboro Patriot*, June 15, 1910.

100. "Moonshine Romantic If Not Respectable," *Winston-Salem Journal*, May 9, 1920.

101. "Federal Prohibition Amendment Ratified by Senate with Practically No Opposition," *News and Observer*, January 11, 1919; "North Carolina Joins Other States of the Union for Amendment," *News and Observer*, January 15, 1919.

102. "An Act to Make the State Law Conform to the National Law in Relation to Intoxicating Liquors." *Public Laws and Resolutions Passed by the General Assembly at Its Session [1923]*, ch. 1, 55–62, accessed February 2, 2021, http://digital.ncdcr.gov/digital/collection/p249901coll22/id/236227.

103. Wickersham Commission, *Enforcement of the Prohibition Laws*. (Washington, D.C.: U.S. Government Printing Office, 1931), 738.

104. Wickersham Commission, *Enforcement*, 739.

105. "Seize Beer Load," *Greensboro Record*, January 26, 1931.

106. "Sheriff Busy in September," *Greensboro Record*, October 3, 1932.

107. "Bootleggerette Is Captured with Cargo of Whisky," *Greensboro Record*, January 4, 1933.

108. "The Paramount Issue," *Greensboro Record*, August 16, 1932.

109. "An Act to Legalize the Sale of Beer, Ale, Porter, and Fruit Juices," *Public Laws and Resolutions Passed by the General Assembly at Its Session [1933]*, ch. 216, 335–37, accessed February 2, 2021, http://digital.ncdcr.gov/digital/collection/p249901coll22/id/241739/rec/1.

110. "Legal Beer to Flow in North Carolina," *Greensboro Record*, April 6, 1933.

111. "One Year of Beer," *Greensboro Record*, May 3, 1934.

112. "An Act to Provide for the Calling of a Convention of the People of North Carolina for the Purpose of Considering the Proposed Amendment to the Constitution of the United States Repealing the Eighteenth Amendment," *Public Laws and Resolutions passed by the General Assembly at Its Session [1933]*, ch. 403, 600–607, accessed February 2, 2021, http://digital.ncdcr.gov/digital/collection/p249901coll22/id/241739/rec/1.

113. "Repeal Seekers Hold Conference," *News and Observer*, June 8, 1933.

114. *North Carolina Manual* (Raleigh: North Carolina Historical Commission, 1935), 112–13, accessed February 2, 2021, http://babel.hathitrust.org/cgi/pt?id=uc1.b4046905&view=1up&seq=3.

115. "An Act to Provide for and to Regulate the Manufacture, Transportation, and Sale of Malt, Brewed, and Fermented Beverages," *Public Laws and Resolutions Passed by the General Assembly at Its Session [1935]*, ch. 134, 149, accessed February 2, 2021, http://digital.ncdcr.gov/digital/collection/p249901coll22/id/240422.

116. "An Act to Provide for the Manufacture, Sale, and Control of Alcoholic Beverages in North Carolina," *Public Laws and Resolutions Passed by the General Assembly at its Session [1936–1937]*, ch. 49, 84–97, accessed February 2, 2021, http://digital.ncdcr.gov/digital/collection/p249901coll22/id/298111/rec/1.

117. "Economic Data on North Carolina Beer," *Statesville Daily Record*, February 21, 1939.

4. Big Beer Comes to the Triad

118. Advertisement, *Greensboro Daily News*, April 27, 1936; Advertisement, *Greensboro Daily News*, February 26, 1936.

119. Advertisement, *Greensboro Daily News*, April 4, 1936.

120. Advertisement, *Greensboro Daily News*, March 20, 1936.

121. "City Votes for ABC Stores," *Greensboro Daily News*, June 6, 1951; "Corner Store," Triad Municipal ABC Board, accessed February 2, 2021, http://triadabc.wpengine.com/board-history/.

122. "Our History," R.H Barringer, accessed February 2, 2021, https://rhbarringer.com/who-we-are; Advertisement, *Greensboro Daily News*, June 15, 1934.

123. "Our History," I.H. Caffey, accessed February 2, 2021, http://www.caffeydist.com/history/.

124. "City News," *Greensboro Daily News*, January 27, 1935.

125. "Brewery Will Open in Guilford County," *Charlotte Observer*, January 27, 1935.

126. "Beerish," 1967 Dave Phillips Collection Scrapbook, Heritage Research Center at High Point Public Library, accessed February 2, 2021, http://lib.digitalnc.org/record/102748?ln=en#?c=0&m=0&s=0&cv=124&r=0&xywh=5918%2C4245%2C2006%2C1219.

127. "Anheuser Busch, Inc. Plans Brewery Here," *Greensboro Daily News*, May 3, 1967.

128. "Officials Deny Blocks to Brewery," *High Point Enterprise*, August 31, 1967.

129. "Brewery Plans Here Unchanged," *Greensboro Daily News*, September 28, 1967.

130. "Brewery Plans Are Postponed," *High Point Enterprise*, December 22, 1967.

131. "Company Postpones Brewery Construction," *Greensboro Daily News*, December 22, 1967.

132. "Piedmont Crescent Approaching Crisis," *High Point Enterprise*, December 3, 1972.

133. "Anheuser Busch, Inc. Plans Brewery Here," *Greensboro Daily News*, May 3, 1967.

134. "Brewery Set for Winston Area," *Daily Times-News*, June 30, 1967.

135. "Brewery Set for Winston Area."

136. "Schlitz Winston-Salem Is On-Stream," *Modern Brewery Age*, June 22, 1970, 22–28.

137. "Brewery Will Open in Late Summer," *High Point Enterprise*, April 23, 1969.

138. "The New Winston-Salem, NC, Plant of the Jos. Schlitz Brewing Co," *Brewer's Digest*, June 1970, 24–52.

139. "Schlitz Will Build Brewery at Winston," 1967 Dave Phillips Collection Scrapbook, Heritage Research Center at High Point Public Library, accessed February 2, 2021, http://lib.digitalnc.org/record/102748?ln=en#?c=0&m=0&s=0&cv=124&r=0&xywh=5918%2C4245%2C2006%2C1219.

140. "Jos. Schlitz Brewing Co.," *Winston-Salem and Vicinity Visitor Attractions*, 1970, 7, in Boonville Extension Homemakers Club Scrapbook, Yadkin County Public Library, accessed February 2, 2021, http://lib.digitalnc.org/record/106321#?c=0&m=0&s=0&cv=45&r=0&xywh=-483%2C-1%2C4642%2C2830.

141. "Schlitz Winston-Salem Is On-Stream," *Modern Brewery Age*, June 22, 1970, 22–28.

142. "New Winston-Salem, NC, Plant."

143. "Brewery Picks Teamsters," *Daily Times-News*, September 20, 1969.

144. Brian Louis, "Winston-Salem, N.C., Brewery Sells for $19.3 Million," *Winston-Salem Journal*, August 1, 2003.

145. Michael R. Reilly, "Joseph Schlitz Brewing Co.: A Chronological History 1969-1982," Sussex-Lisbon Area Historical Society, Inc., accessed February 2, 2021, https://web.archive.org/web/20101101132446/http://www.slahs.org/schlitz/history6.htm.

146. Reilly, "Joseph Schlitz Brewing Co."

147. Martyn Cornell, "How Milwaukee's Famous Beer Became Infamous: The Fall of Schlitz," *Beer Connoisseur*, January 10, 2010, accessed February 2, 2021, http://beerconnoisseur.com/articles/how-milwaukees-famous-beer-became-infamous.

148. Cornell, "How Milwaukee's Famous Beer Became Infamous."

149. "Oh Schlitz! 3 Lessons on Cutting Corners," *EduCred Services*, June 24, 2015, accessed February 2, 2021, http://educredservices.com/blog/2015/6/24/oh-schlitz-3-lessons-on-cutting-corners.

150. Cornell, "How Milwaukee's Famous Beer Became Infamous."

151. Cornell, "How Milwaukee's Famous Beer Became Infamous."

152. Reilly, "Joseph Schlitz Brewing Co."

153. Louis, "Winston-Salem, N.C. Brewery Sells."

154. Eleni Chamis, "Stroh to Sell Beer Brands," *Winston-Salem Journal*, February 9, 1999.

155. Jane Seccombe, "Last Call for a Stroh's; Brewery Prepares to Close, Ending 30 Years in Winston," *Winston-Salem Journal*, August 4, 1999.

156. Louis, "Winston-Salem, N.C. Brewery Sells for $19.3 Million."

157. Seccombe, "Last Call for a Stroh's."

158. "Miller Brewery Started at Eden," *High Point Enterprise*, June 30, 1976.

159. "Miller's History in Eden Progresses," *Greensboro Daily News*, March 26, 1978.

160. "Eden Likely to Get Miller Plant," *The Robesonian*, May 31, 1976.

161. "Miller's Projections for 36 Million Capacity Seen Completed by 1980," *Modern Brewery Age*, August 8, 1977, 58–59.

162. "Miller Brewery Started at Eden."

163. "Brewery Opposed," *Statesville Record and Landmark*, January 28, 1976.

164. "Miller's History in Eden Progresses."

165. "Miller's Projections," *Modern Brewery Age*.

166. "Production Started," *Greensboro Record*, March 24, 1978.

167. Tad Stewart, "Teamsters Win Vote at Miller," *Greensboro Daily News*, May 26, 1978.

168. "Miller Brewery Construction Almost Complete," *Greensboro Daily News*, October 1, 1978.

169. Tad Stewart, "Miller Expansion Means More North Carolina Jobs," *Greensboro Daily News*, October 13, 1979

170. Leslie Brown, "A Brewing Story: Woman's Career Is Beer," *Greensboro News and Record*, August 7, 2000.

171. "Women Bosses in Male Domains," *Ebony*, October 1995, 44–50.

172. "Women Bosses in Male Domains."

173. Arthur O. Murray, "Brew Mistress," *Business North Carolina*, July 2002, 28–33.

174. Murray, "Brew Mistress."

175. Murray, "Brew Mistress."

176. Brown, "Brewing Story."

177. Brown, "Brewing Story."

178. Murray, "Brew Mistress."

179. Murray, "Brew Mistress."

180. Brown, "Brewing Story."

181. Murray, "Brew Mistress."

182. Murray, "Brew Mistress."

183. Matt Evans, "Expansion Shows MillerCoors Remains Committed to Eden," *Triad Business Journal*, January 14, 2011, accessed February 2, 2021, http://www.bizjournals.com/triad/print-edition/2011/01/14/expansion-shows-millercoors-remains.html.

184. Tara Nurin, "It's Final: AB InBev Closes on Deal to Buy SABMiller," *Forbes*, October 10, 2016, accessed February 2, 2021, http://www.forbes.com/sites/taranurin/2016/10/10/its-final-ab-inbev-closes-on-deal-to-buy-sabmiller/?sh=1615990432c8.

185. Richard Craver, "MillerCoors to Close Eden Brewery in September 2016," *Winston-Salem Journal*, September 14, 2015, accessed February 2, 2021, http://journalnow.com/business/business_news/local/millercoors-to-close-eden-brewery-in-september/article_030e463b-1002-530e-abee-d552d420bfdc.html.

186. Craver, "MillerCoors to Close Eden Brewery."

187. Richard Craver, "Purina to Move into Old MillerCoors Plant in Eden," *Winston-Salem Journal*, September 30, 2020, accessed February 2, 2021, http://greensboro.com/rockingham_now/news/purina-to-move-into-old-millercoors-plant-in-eden-300-workers-will-be-needed-for/article_eba652b8-034f-11eb-9608-7bb18e224b33.html.

188. John Harry, "Jimmy Carter: American Homebrew Hero?" National Museum of American History blog, September 30, 2019, accessed February 2, 2021, https://americanhistory.si.edu/blog/papazian.

189. "An Act to Amend the Internal Revenue Code of 1954 with Respect to Excise Tax on Certain Trucks, Buses, Tractors, Et Cetera, Home Production of Beer and Wine, Refunds of the Taxes on Gasoline and Special Fuels to Aerial Applicators, and Partial Rollovers of Lump Sum Distributions," 95th Congress (1977–78), accessed February 2, 2021, http://www.congress.gov/bill/95th-congress/house-bill/1337/summary.

190. "Historical U.S. Brewery Count," *Brewers Association*, accessed February 2, 2021, https://www.brewersassociation.org/statistics-and-data/national-beer-stats/.

5. The Brewpub Boom

191. Uli Bennewitz, interview by Richard Cox, August 17, 2018, Well Crafted NC, UNC Greensboro University Libraries.

192. Bennewitz, interview.

193. "S.B. 536: An Act to Allow On-Premise Sales of Beer at Mini-Breweries," North Carolina General Assembly, accessed February 2, 2021, http://www.ncleg.gov/BillLookup/1985/sb536.

194. William Cissna, "Out and About: Loggerhead Brewing Company," *All About Beer*, October/November 1990, 40.

195. Leigh Pressley, "Stirring Up a Brew: Vickers Beer Served Fresh from the Tap," *Greensboro News & Record*, August 5, 1990, accessed February 2, 2021, http://greensboro.com/stirring-up-a-brew-vickers-beer-served-fresh-from-the/article_114d4ebe-606b-5606-8133-48693a536f2b.html.

196. John Batchelor, "Here's a Hearty Snub to Standard Pub Grub," *Greensboro News & Record*, August 13, 1992, accessed February 2, 2021, http://greensboro.com/here-s-a-hearty-snub-to-standard-pub-grub/article_65f0cfb5-f515-5b8d-9477-da54ff95f0f4.html; Loggerhead Brewing Company Menu, Richard Cox Personal Collection, accessed February 2, 2021, http://libcdm1.uncg.edu/cdm/ref/collection/Community/id/4918.

197. Bill Sugg, "Greensboro Breweries Are at the Head of the Class," *Greensboro News & Record*, April 26, 1995, accessed February 2, 2021, https://greensboro.com/greensboro-breweries-are-at-head-of-class/article_30a554fd-3a8c-5629-aa75-0fb19c5d994f.html.

198. Loggerhead Brewing Company Menu.

199. Mark Folk, "Brewery Will Close Restaurant Loggerhead Brewing Co.," *Greensboro News & Record*, April 8, 1994, accessed February 2, 2021, http://greensboro.com/brewery-will-close-restaurant-loggerhead-brewing-co/article_17e1cb73-6847-5943-8125-a1419501ad1a.html.

200. Sugg, "Greensboro Breweries Are at the Head."

201. Sugg, "Greensboro Breweries Are at the Head"; Virginia Thomas, "Spring Garden," *New Brewer*, May/June 1992, 44.

202. Thomas, "Spring Garden," 44.

203. Thomas, "Spring Garden," 46.

204. "Newly Named Pub Deserves a Second Look," *Greensboro News & Record*, June 20. 2001, accessed February 2, 2021, http://greensboro.com/newly-named-pub-deserves-a-second-look/article_06cf9b37-bef9-5b20-9bbd-570035e7a3a3.html.

205. Stephen Martin, "Big Changes Brewing for Beer Maker," *Greensboro News & Record*, August 3, 2002, accessed February 2, 2021, http://greensboro.com/big-changes-brewing-for-beer-maker-spring-garden-brewing-co/article_24811eb3-f7b1-53ec-9ee4-aa708e2cb284.html; Lex Alexander, "More Beer, Tanks," *Greensboro News & Record*, April 10, 2007, accessed February 2, 2021, https://greensboro.com/news/general_assignment/more-beer-tanks/article_06618094-4889-5806-9aa5-2ac76afc55c0.html.

206. Debra D. Bass, "New Steakhouse Plans Eight Brews of Its Own Design," *Greensboro News & Record*, October 26, 1999, accessed February 2, 2021, http://greensboro.com/new-steakhouse-plans-eight-brews-of-its-own-design-a-new-restaurant-wants-to-liberate/article_b0d2fa8f-8b58-594f-8267-24f657ad08c6.html.

207. Erik Lars Myers and Sarah H. Ficke, *North Carolina Craft Beer & Breweries*, 2nd ed. (Winston-Salem, NC: John F. Blair Publisher, 2016), 189–91.

208. Matt Harrington, "Microbrewery Is on Tap for Downtown GSO: Serving the Greater Triad Area," *Business Journal*, October 17, 2003.

209. Kayne Fisher, interview by Brandi Ragghianti, October 2, 2017, Well Crafted NC, UNC Greensboro University Libraries.

210. "Business Doings," *News and Observer*, October 14, 2006.

211. Matt Harrington, "Brew Pub Gets Green Light in Winston-Salem," *Business Journal*, February 6, 2004.

212. Jeff Smith, "New Places to Eat and Drink Downtown Are on the Horizon," *Winston-Salem Journal*, March 10, 2005.

213. Tony Kiss, "Head for the Hills for Some Award-Winning Brews," *Asheville Citizen-Times*, May 7, 2008.

214. Kiss, "Head for the Hills"; Jamie Bartholomaus, interview by Richard Cox, May 15, 2018, Well Crafted NC, UNC Greensboro University Libraries.

215. Lorraine Ahearn, "Bargain Beer Takes Some Patience," *Greensboro News & Record*, November 3, 1993, accessed February 2, 2021, http://greensboro.com/bargain-beer-takes-some-patience/article_bbefc999-7c5b-5715-906a-59be17313185.html.

216. Robert Lopez, "The Homebrew Crew," *Winston-Salem Monthly*, December 26, 2017, accessed February 2, 2021, http://journalnow.com/winstonsalemmonthly/the-homebrew-crew/article_e4b8ccda-ea7d-11e7-8c6d-63abdfac3940.html; "About Us," Battleground Brewers Guild, accessed February 2, 2021, http://www.battlegroundbrewers.com/about.

217. Fisher, interview.

218. Doug Campbell, "Beer Nuts," *Triad Business Journal*, January 3, 2000, accessed February 2, 2021, http://www.bizjournals.com/triangle/stories/2000/01/03/smallb1.html; Paul Nowell, "No Ordinary Brew: Greensboro Beer Distributor Specializes in Microbrews," *Greensboro News & Record*, June 15, 1997, accessed February 2, 2021, http://greensboro.com/no-ordinary-brew-greensboro-beer-distributor-specializes-in-microbrews/article_efbce837-d38f-5c76-874f-ebc042e7fc65.html.

219. Matt Harrington, "Developers Eye New Projects in Downtown GSO: Serving the Greater Triad Area," *Triad Business Journal*, March 5, 2004.

220. Joe Gamm, "Popular Beer Festival A Draw for the Stouts," *Greensboro News & Record*, July 13, 2014, accessed February 2, 2021, http://greensboro.com/popular-beer-festival-a-draw-for-the-stout/article_bcc97d10-295c-58cd-a6e2-66f24e68904e.html.

221. Jeff Smith, "Inaugural Festival for Beer Lovers to Be Held Saturday," *Winston-Salem Journal*, July 28, 2005.

222. Denise Becker, "It Was a Beery Good Year," *Greensboro News & Record*, March 12, 2002, accessed February 2, 2021, http://greensboro.com/it-was-a-beery-good-year-the-first-woman-crowned-beer-drinker-of-the-year/article_ffa85b84-f4c9-5ae4-98e2-0c85a65d96ee.html; Michael Hastings, "The Beer Is Ready, Now It's Time to Party," *Winston-Salem Journal*, August 28, 2013, accessed February 2, 2021, https://journalnow.com/lifestyles/food/hastings-the-beer-is-ready-now-its-time-for-a-party/article_ffff2436-0f70-11e3-aedc-001a4bcf6878.html.

223. Pop the Cap fundraising letter, March 13, 2005, Pop the Cap Archives, University of North Carolina at Greensboro, University Libraries, accessed February 2, 2021, http://libcdm1.uncg.edu/cdm/singleitem/collection/Community/id/2712/rec/1.

224. Myers and Ficke, *North Carolina Craft Beer*, 222–23.

225. Kathleen Purvis, "NC Craft Beer Industry Now Tops in the South," *Raleigh News & Observer*, August 8, 2015, accessed February 2, 2021, http://www.newsobserver.com/news/local/article30529083.html.

6. Craft Beer in the Triad Today

226. Catherine Carlock, "Triad Boosts Business of Beer with Craft Breweries," *Triad Business Journal*, October 18, 2013, accessed February 2, 2021, http://www.bizjournals.com/triad/print-edition/2013/10/18/triad-boosts-business-of-beer-with.html.

227 "Tracing the History of 'Shine' in Randolph County," *Courier-Tribune*, November 17, 2014, accessed February 2, 2021, http://www.courier-tribune.com/article/20141117/NEWS/311179757.

228. "Voters OK Sale of Alcohol in Asheboro," *Winston-Salem Journal*, July 30, 2008, accessed February 2, 2021, http://journalnow.com/news/local/voters-ok-sale-of-alcohol-in-asheboro/article_1788136a-6ff8-51a4-bc30-41bd3c7bb84f.html.

229. Catherine Carlock, "Drink Up, Entrepreneurs: Downtown Greensboro Now Allows Microbreweries," *Triad Business Journal*, February 21, 2014, http://www.bizjournals.com/triad/blog/2014/02/drink-up-entrepreneurs-downtown.html.

230. "Amending Chapter 30 (LDO): An Ordinance Amending the Greensboro Code of Ordinances with Respect to Zoning, Planning, and Development," February 8, 2014, accessed February 2, 2021, http://www.greensboro-nc.gov/modules/showdocument.aspx?documentid=23158.

231. Joe Dexter, "RCC Crafts Classes for Brewers," *Greensboro News & Record*, March 27, 2017, accessed February 2, 2021, http://greensboro.com/rockingham_now/news/rcc-crafts-classes-for-brewers/article_0726214e-022d-11e7-b980-ef42e09739a0.html.

232. Carlock, "Triad Boosts Business of Beer."

233. Todd Isbell, interview by Richard Cox, August 9, 2019, Well Crafted NC, UNC Greensboro University Libraries.

234. Isbell, interview.

235. Dexter, "RCC Crafts Classes for Brewers."

236. "About Us," Radar Brewing Company home page, accessed February 2, 2021, https://www.radarbrewingcompany.com/about-us.

237. Myers and Ficke, *North Carolina Craft Beer*, 214.

238. Michael Hastings, "Brewery Has Endured Fire and COVID-19 on Its Way to Becoming Lexington's First for Craft Beer," *Winston-Salem Journal*, June 9, 2020, accessed February 2, 2021, http://journalnow.com/entertainment/dining/brewery-has-endured-fire-and-covid-19-on-its-way-to-becoming-lexingtons-first-for/article_0a8721e1-4c17-59f1-a118-4c2f0ad1b4e5.html.

239. "Triad Brewers Alliance (TBA) Tripel," Four Saints Brewing Company, accessed February 2, 2021, http://www.foursaintsbrewing.com/triad-brewers-alliance-tba-tripel.

240. Downtown Taste n Tap, "Who Was the Winner," Facebook, June 9, 2018, accessed February 2, 2021, http://www.facebook.com/events/1813240298728695/?active_tab=discussion.

241. Joel McClosky, interview by Richard Cox, October 24, 2018, Well Crafted NC, UNC Greensboro University Libraries.

242. Erik Lars Myers and Sarah H. Ficke, *North Carolina Craft Beer and Breweries*, 192-193.

243. McClosky, interview.

244. Lex Alexander, "More Tanks, Please," *Greensboro News and Record*, April 10, 2007, accessed February 2, 2021, http://greensboro.com/news/general_assignment/more-beer-tanks/article_06618094-4889-5806-9aa5-2ac76afc55c0.html.

245. Carl Wilson, "Red Oak Brewery Opens Beer Hall," *Winston-Salem Journal*, December 15, 2017, accessed February 2, 2021, http://journalnow.com/home_food/food/red-oak-brewery-opens-beer-hall/article_54bf3906-0efb-52ca-80a4-c5a7b20f1c53.html.

246. John Brasier, "First Look: Inside Natty Greene's Kitchen + Market at Revolution Mill," *Greensboro News and Record*, June 15, 2017, accessed February 2, 2021, http://www.bizjournals.com/triad/news/2017/06/15/first-look-inside-natty-greenes-kitchen-market-at.html.

247. Richard Barron, "Natty's Owners Vow to Keep Greensboro Restaurant Open as Brewery Files for Chapter 7 Bankruptcy," *Greensboro News and Record*, October 21, 2020, accessed February 2, 2021, http://greensboro.com/business/nattys-owners-vow-to-keep-greensboro-restaurant-open-as-brewery-files-for-chapter-7-bankruptcy/article_b195116c-13d1-11eb-9ec3-0bc488dae7f3.html.

248. John Braiser, "Joymongers Planning New Concept for Location in Winston-Salem," *Triad Business Journal*, August 28, 2017, accessed February 2, 2021, http://www.bizjournals.com/triad/news/2017/08/28/joymongers-planning-new-concept-for-2nd-location.html; Jane Little,

"Here's a Look Inside the New Joymongers Barrel Hall in Winston-Salem," *Triad Business Journal*, March 16, 2018, accessed February 2, 2021, http://www.bizjournals.com/triad/news/2018/03/16/heres-a-look-inside-the-new-joymongers-barrel-hall.html.

249. Nicole Preyer, interview with Erin Lawrimore, August 28. 2018, Well Crafted NC, UNC Greensboro University Libraries.

250. "Fighting Fear with Beer: Virus Spurs Curbside Beer Sales," *USA Today*, March 18, 2020, accessed February 2, 2021, http://www.usnews.com/news/business/articles/2020-03-18/fighting-fear-with-beer-virus-spurs-curbside-beer-sales.

251. Hastings, "Brewery Has Endured Fire and COVID-19."

252. Sayaka Matsuoka, "'If People Need It, We'll Do It': Local Breweries Start Offering Delivery," *Triad City Beat*, April 3, 2020, accessed February 2, 2021, http://triad-city-beat.com/local-breweries-delivery.

253. "COVID-19 Resource Page," North Carolina Craft Brewers Guild, accessed February 2, 2021, http://www.ncbeer.org/covid-19_resource_page.php.

254. Daniel Finnegan, "Gibb's Hundred Brewing Company Closes Its Doors," *Triad Business Journal*, September 15, 2020, accessed February 2, 2021, http://www.bizjournals.com/triad/news/2020/09/15/gibbs-hundred-brewing-company-closes.html.

255. Gibb's Hundred Brewing Company, "On Sunday, September 13th at 8pm, We Will Have One Final 'Last Call'," Facebook, September 8, 2020, accessed February 2, 2021, http://www.facebook.com/gibbshundred/photos/a.703121103032338/3661102197234199/?type=3.

256. John Brasier, "Greensboro Brewpub Will Spend $800K on Renovations," *Triad Business Journal*, November 4, 2019, accessed February 2, 2021, http://www.bizjournals.com/triad/news/2019/11/04/greensboro-brewpub-will-spend-800k-on-renovations.html.

257. "Statement from ACC on Men's Basketball Tournament," Atlantic Coast Conference, March 12, 2020, accessed February 2, 2021, http://theacc.com/news/2020/3/12/statement-from-acc-on-mens-basketball-tournament.aspx.

258. Natty Greene's Brewhouse, "We Are Closing Our Brewhouse Location on Gate City Blvd Indefinitely Due to the Pandemic," Facebook, October 8, 2020, http://www.facebook.com/NGBrewhouse/photos/a.236883855 3218250/3024594664309299/?type=3.

259. Barron, "Natty's Owners Vow to Keep Greensboro."

260. "SouthEnd Brewing Partners with Natty Greene's to Keep Original Recipes Alive," WFMY News 2, November 20, 2020, accessed February 2, 2021, http://www.wfmynews2.com/video/news/local/south-end-brewing-natty-greenes-brewing-company-downtown-greensboro-helping-each-other-partnering/83-c209d5f4-9623-4c4f-b337-fc33602a2eee.

INDEX

ABOUT THE AUTHORS

The authors are the co-founders of Well Crafted NC (www. WellCraftedNC.com), a project focused on documenting the history of beer and brewing in North Carolina. They all work in the University Libraries at the University of North Carolina–Greensboro.

In addition to researching and visiting craft breweries, RICHARD COX (*right*) spends his spare time reading, drawing and collecting vintage Japanese kaiju toys. DAVID GWYNN (*left*) is obsessed with shawarma, supermarket history, cities and buildings and almost anything Canadian. ERIN LAWRIMORE (*middle*) is passionate about archival outreach, dogs and animal rescue and coffee.

Visit us at
www.historypress.com